WORLD RELIGIONS SERIES
Series Editor: W. Owen Cole

CW00371504

Islam

Syed Ali Ashraf

Stanley Thornes (Publishers) Ltd

First published in 1991 by:
Stanley Thornes (Publishers) Ltd
Ellenborough House
Wellington Street
CHELTENHAM GL50 1YD
England

Reprinted 1994

British Library Cataloguing in Publication Data

Ashraf, Syed Ali
 Islam. – (World religions)
 I. Title   II. Series
 297.07

ISBN 1–871402–10–7

Typeset by Tech-Set, Gateshead, Tyne & Wear.
Printed and bound in Great Britain at The Bath Press, Avon.

Acknowledgements

I thank all scholars, teachers, friends and students with whom I have had seminars, discussions and classroom work on the teaching of Islam in British schools. My special thanks are due to Dr Owen Cole for his very practical and useful guidance, to Dr Abdul Mabud for helping to prepare the index and illustrations on pp. 6, 29 and 31 and for some valuable comments, to Mo Sylvester for typing, and to my wife for constant support and encouragement.

Syed Ali Ashraf

The author and publishers are grateful to the following for permission to use and reproduce photographs:

Mrs Selina Ali, pp. 80, 81, 102; Mrs Ayesha Gouverneur, pp. 4, 13, 20, 23 (both), 43, 47, 61 (both), 63, 64 (all), 66, 68 (all), 78, 79 (both), 83, 100, 107, 110, 122; Ann and Bury Peerless, p. 123; Peter Sanders, pp. 11, 34, 48, 86, 90 (both), 95, 127.

Every effort has been made to contact copyright holders of photographs used in this book, and we apologise if any have been overlooked.

Extracts from 'The World's Classics' *The Koran Interpreted* by Arthur J. Arberry are reproduced by kind permission of HarperCollins Publishers Ltd.

The cover photographs show: (top right) Woman praying on decorative prayer carpet; (centre) the Ka'ba; (bottom left) the Regent's Park Mosque; (bottom right) illuminated manuscript of the Qur'ān.

A note on language

To help students pronounce correctly the Arabic words used in this book, three diacritical marks are used:

' to indicate a glottal stop, as in *Qur'ān*,

' to indicate a strong guttural sound produced in the throat and by breathing out, as in *Rabī'*,

¯ above a, u and i, to make these vowels long, as in *salāh*.

A note on the Qur'ān

The longer extracts quoted in this book are taken from Arberry's *The Koran Interpreted*, but some of the references to single verses or words are from Yusuf Ali's *The Holy Qur'ān, Translation and Commentary* (see Further Reading, p. 137, for bibliographical details). Some of the translations have been glossed by the author.

Contents

Preface

This book attempts to present Islam as a religion followed by a large number of people throughout the world. Though these people speak different languages and have different customs and conventions, they all try to follow a common way of life which they find in Islam. This book does not give a picture of the different ways of living of these various groups of people; it attempts to present an accurate and sound overview of the total way of life that Islam wants people to follow.

Over a period of 1400 years, it is hardly surprising that different schools of thought and different sorts of cultural expression of Islam have developed in different parts of the world. It is, however, remarkable that the basic beliefs and practices and the ethical conduct of the followers of this religion, Muslims, have remained the same. Minor sects have emerged and vanished. This book does not deal with their sectarian beliefs and practices. It tries to present the main stream of thought. The followers of this main stream are known as Sunnis. They form nearly 90 per cent of the Muslim population of the world. Leaving aside the minor sects, the major portion of the rest of the Muslim population are known as Shi'as. There is no difference between the major beliefs and practices of these two groups. The differences in their interpretations of Islam are indicated in this book.

Islamic beliefs and practices are completely integrated with the life and habits of a Muslim. A non-Muslim will not appreciate this total way of life unless he or she knows the role that the Qur'ān, the holy book of the Muslims, and the life and instructions of the Prophet who preached this religion, play in a Muslim's life. A Muslim will never utter the name of the Prophet without at the same time saying, 'May the blessings of God be on him' or simply 'Peace be upon him'. That is why throughout this book, whenever the Prophet's name Muhammad occurs, the words 'peace be upon him' are used after his name. It is printed in an abbreviated form: 'pbuh'. This is also the custom when a Muslim utters the name of any of the earlier prophets. A Muslim has deep reverence for all the prophets and never dares to criticise any one of them.

In the final chapter of this book an attempt has been made to present to students the relevance of Islam in today's world. Although a positive conclusion is presented, students are encouraged to reflect on the questions raised and to draw their own conclusions.

Throughout the book the words God and Allah are used as interchangeable terms. Some scholars do not like this, but I believe that in so far as the essence of God is concerned, all great religions believe it to be Unique, Incomparable, Unknowable and eternally the same. He is without a beginning and without an end. Though we use the masculine pronoun 'He' for God, He is neither masculine nor feminine. All that can be said is: 'He is He and nothing else.'

Syed Ali Ashraf

Chapter 1

Introduction:
Islam and the Muslims

The map (below) shows that there is a large chunk of land in Africa and Asia occupied mainly by people who are known as Muslims. Muslims now form the largest religious minority in Britain. They have also migrated to many countries in Europe, particularly to France, Germany and Holland. History books dealing with the thirteenth and fourteenth centuries and even up to the nineteenth century reveal that there was a huge Muslim Empire occupying nearly the whole of what is now known as eastern Europe, including Poland, Czechoslovakia, Hungary, Romania, Yugoslavia, Bulgaria, Albania, Greece, and even portions of the USSR. For nearly four and a half centuries the whole of Spain was ruled by the Muslims. A wonderful civilisation flourished in Cordoba in southern Spain. Through the works of the Muslim philosophers, Avecina and Averroes (Ibn Sina and Ibn Rushd), the works of Greek philosophers – especially Plato and Aristotle – came to be appreciated by Latin scholars in Europe during the thirteenth and fourteenth

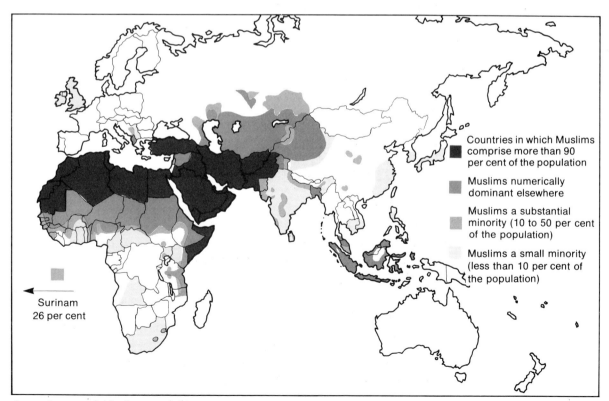

Countries in which Muslims comprise more than 90 per cent of the population

Muslims numerically dominant elsewhere

Muslims a substantial minority (10 to 50 per cent of the population)

Muslims a small minority (less than 10 per cent of the population)

Surinam
26 per cent

Present areas of Muslim population

centuries. European historians describe this as the source of a new revival of learning in Europe. Then, in the late fifteenth century, the Muslim rulers were defeated and a large number of Muslims were driven out or killed.

Since the Crusades there has often been a misunderstanding and a wrong presentation of Islam. Now that Muslims are living in Britain, non-Muslims need to get an accurate picture of these people and their religion. As their religion provides Muslims with a complete way of life, it is necessary for everyone to understand what Islam means and how its followers live, what they believe in and how they work according to their beliefs, what heritage they have and how their beliefs are utilised for the benefit of themselves and the country as a whole.

WHAT IS ISLAM?

Islam is the name of the religion that Muslims follow. 'Islam' is an Arabic word. In Arabic, clusters of words come from particular roots. Islam comes from the root 'slm', from which also come words meaning 'surrender' and 'peace'. Islam means 'peace through surrender to God'. It is a way of obedience.

The Arabic word for religion is *dīn*. It refers to a complete way of life from birth to death and even to life after death. It tells those who accept it what they should believe, how they should behave with other human beings, with all other living creatures and also with all natural objects so that they may obtain spiritual peace through obeying God's Will.

The word 'Muslim' also comes from the same root 'slm'. It means one who has submitted or surrendered him- or herself to God.

The Central Tenet of Islam

The central tenet of this religion is brief and simple. The following Arabic sentence sums up the whole *dīn*:

lā ilāha illallāhu Muhammadur Rasūlullāh

It means: There is no god but God and Muhammad is His Messenger.

It implies: There is no one worthy of worship except God and God has sent Muhammad (pbuh) to convey His message to humanity.

There is no Divinity but that of God and He has revealed to human beings that way of life which is good for them through His chosen person, Prophet Muhammad (pbuh). In order to live this way of life, therefore, a person must follow Muhammad (pbuh). In order to follow him, one must know him, understand him, obey him and love him. God tells the Prophet to tell all Muslims, 'If you love God then follow me, then God will love you.'

Islam as 'The' World Religion

Muslims believe that God sent only one religion for human beings. All of God's messengers or prophets preached in essence the same religion – the same way of life and the same code of conduct. All the prophets and all those who believe in them are therefore Muslims. All religions are thus the same 'religion of surrender to God'. From this point of view, Muslims believe all religions were originally Islam.

As time went on, however, the followers of earlier prophets began to alter, modify and suppress what had been revealed by God to His messengers or prophets. Muslims believe in all the prophets and consider them as prophets of Islam, as well as Muhammad (pbuh). Other prophets, using the names by which they are best known in the west, include: Abraham, Ishmael, Moses, Joseph, David and Jesus.

Belief in all the prophets
God tells the Muslims that the believers should say: 'We make no division [distinction] between any one of His Messengers.' (Qur'ān, 2:285).

When Muslims look at the similarities which exist between such religions as Judaism, Christianity and Islam, they say that this is because the religions all came from the same source – the message which God gave the prophets. Islam, therefore, is the name of the religion of God for all human beings.

The Last Revealed Religion

'Revealed' religions are those which were 'revealed' or sent to humankind by God. Muslims believe that Islam, as preached by the Prophet Muhammad (pbuh), is the last revealed religion. The first prophet was Adam, the first human being created by God. Muhammad (pbuh) was the last prophet. He was chosen by God to purify the message He had sent to earlier prophets, such as Moses, because, as we have seen, the followers of these earlier prophets later modified, changed, added to or suppressed the actual message received by the prophets. Again and again people forgot God's instructions and went away from the path of goodness. They set up many gods and goddesses and started worshipping them, sometimes along with God.

The followers of the prophet Jesus, who lived 570 years before Muhammad (pbuh), came to be known as Christians. People began to worship Jesus. Many different sects emerged, and his message became distorted. Muslims therefore believe that it was necessary for God to choose a new prophet to send to the world so that the original religion as preached by Abraham, Moses and Jesus could again be followed by believers. Muhammad (pbuh) was that person.

Muslims believe that Muhammad (pbuh) is the last prophet and that the message revealed to him is God's final word to humanity. In the nineteenth century Mirza Golam Ahmad of Qadian in India (now part of Pakistan) claimed to be a prophet. Orthodox Islam cannot accept this view or recognise his followers to be Muslims, even though they use the Qur'ān as their holy book.

MUSLIMS AND BELIEVERS IN OTHER RELIGIONS

If Islam is *the* purified form of God's message for human beings, if it is *the* true religion, the *dīn* as the Qur'ān says, then what is the attitude of Muslims to believers in other religions? The answer to this question is to be found both in the Qur'ān and also in the way Muslims have treated believers in other religions.

The Qur'ān invites all human beings to accept Islam. To those who do not accept it, the Qur'ān tells Muslims to say 'To you your religion, and to me my religion!' (Qur'ān, 109:6). In other words, the Qur'ān instructs Muslims to tolerate and give freedom to each individual to have his or her own faith.

The history of Muslim rule in the world also tells us that Jews, Christians, Hindus, Buddhists and followers of all other religions were allowed to practise their faiths. They were allowed to have their own schools and publish their own literature. There was no imposition of nationally determined curricula and textbooks. The main reason for this was that there was no concept of nationalism. People belonged to their respective religious groups and to tribes or races. The situation is more complicated today because we are supposed to belong first to a particular nation and then to a religious or other group.

HISTORICAL BACKGROUND

Islam was first preached in Arabia, now known as Saudi Arabia. If you look on the map (p. 5) you will see three cities, Makkah (Mecca), Medina and Taif, in a region called the Hijaz. These cities existed in the days of the Prophet. Makkah was the best known of the three because it had been a place of pilgrimage since the time of Abraham. He built the house of God there, known as the Ka'ba. It replaced one which Adam had made but which had later been washed away during the great flood which is linked with the name of Noah. Abraham built the Ka'ba with the help of his son Isma'il (Ishmael). The prophet Muhammad (pbuh), who was a direct descendant of Isma'il, was the first prophet in that line of Abraham's family for 2000 years. Much of his work was that of reminding the Arabs of a religion they had almost forgotten.

The Ka'ba, Makkah, in times past

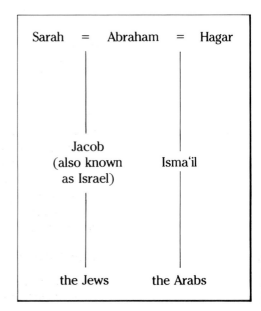

Sarah = Abraham = Hagar

Jacob
(also known
as Israel)   Isma'il

the Jews   the Arabs

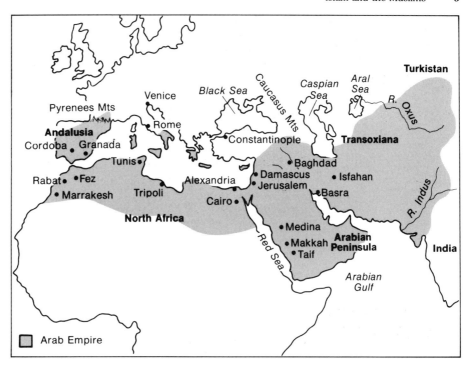

The Arab Empire

Religious and Social Conditions in Arabia

Arabia was a land of many religions at the time of Muhammad's (pbuh) birth. There were Jewish tribes, especially in and around Medina. There were also Christian groups who looked to Constantinople, the centre of the Byzantine Empire, for leadership and protection. Except for a handful of devoted people, these two groups had become this-worldly and materialistic. The nomadic Bedouins had their own gods and goddesses. Although, 2000 years earlier, Abraham and Isma'il (peace be upon them) had preached the message of the One True God, Allah, to the Arabs, most of them had forgotten it and had invented gods and goddesses of their own. Of these the most important were al-Lāt, al-Manāt and al-'Uzza. The statues of the gods and goddesses filled the Ka'ba, the house of God.

Life was often cruel. Girls were considered a burden and many were killed by their parents at birth. No one brought the murderers to justice. Slavery was common. There was no justice for slaves – a master had the right to kill them. Women were not considered to be human beings; they were chattels to be controlled by men. A man could marry as many women as he liked. There was no form of universal justice. The tribal leader was the judge within each tribe, but if a person killed someone belonging to another tribe, the murder could not be judged unless there was some treaty between the tribes. At the same time, within the tribe, there was a high sense of loyalty.

The *Hanīfs*

There were still a few pious, righteous and truthful people. They believed in the One, Unique, Transcendental Deity in the tradition of Abraham. They tended to keep apart from the rest of society. They were sometimes able to influence individuals, but not the powerful tribal rulers. These lonely figures were known as *Hanīf*, meaning upright. One of them was Waraqa bin Nawfal, a cousin of Khadijah, the first wife of Prophet Muhammad (pbuh).

Makkah

The city of Makkah had a unique position. Because of the Ka'ba, it had become the centre of pilgrimage. It was also by far the most important centre for trade and commerce. The tribe that ruled Makkah was known as the Quraysh. There were

The Arabian peninsula showing the main trade route used by the Quraysh tribe

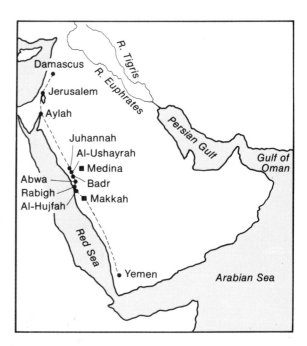

Makkah, at the time of the Prophet and today

several sections of this tribe, belonging to different family heads. The Prophet's family was known as the Hashimites because Hashim was their forefather. The Prophet's grandfather, Abdul Muttalib, was their leader. He was the custodian of the Ka'ba.

It was against this background that Muhammad (pbuh) was born and brought up and received God's message to preach Islam.

?

1 Was Islam known to Europeans before the Crusades? How?
2 Did the western and Islamic civilisations ever have peaceful contacts? When? In what ways?
3 What is the meaning of *dīn*?
4 Do Muslims revere the prophets of Judaism and Jesus? Why?
5 What is the attitude of Muslims towards Jews and Christians?
6 What is the Ka'ba? When was it first built? Who built it? (Look forward to Chapter 15 for more about the Ka'ba.)
7 What was Abraham's contribution to the building of this house of worship?
8 How does the story of the Ka'ba help Muslims to remember that their religion is the one God provided for all humanity?
9 a Do you think the condition of society in Arabia in the sixth century CE was such that there was a need for a new leader, a new prophet? If so, why?
   b Discuss the kinds of qualities such a person would need to bring peace and unity to the region.
10 How would a Muslim define the term 'Muslim' in a few sentences?
11 How is it possible for Muslims to believe that 'all religions were originally Islam'? (see p. 3).

Chapter 2

The Early Life of Muhammad (pbuh)

Muhammad (pbuh) was born in Makkah on Monday, the twelfth day of the lunar month of *Rabī' al-Awwal* in the year 570 CE (Common Era). He was born into the Quraysh tribe. His father Abdullah died a few months before his birth. His mother's name was Amina. He could not enjoy her affection for very long, for she died when he was just six years old. They were returning from Medina where she had gone to visit his father's grave and meet her relatives. On the way home she fell ill and died, and Muhammad (pbuh) became an orphan. A slave girl who was with them took Muhammad (pbuh) back to Makkah, where his grandfather, Abdul Muttalib, took charge of him. Within two years his grandfather had also passed away. Before his death he called one of his sons, Abu Talib, and asked him to take charge of the boy. Till his death Abu Talib protected, guarded and helped Muhammad (pbuh). Thus Muhammad's (pbuh) life began with the sorrows and losses of near and dear ones.

Announcement of his Future

God had made Muhammad (pbuh) suffer these losses, yet at the same time He had sent a message to his mother about his great future. Amina once saw a bright light coming out of her and lighting up the whole world. Some days before her son's birth, she saw an angel in a dream. The angel came down from the sky and told her: 'Glad news to you, O mother of the blessed last prophet. Your son will be the deliverer of humankind. The name decided for him is Ahmad.' She therefore named her son Ahmad, which means 'the most praised one'. After his birth, his grandfather took him to the Ka'ba and named him Muhammad, 'the praised one'. Both words come from the same root. It is the second name by which he is generally known. The name Ahmad also occurs in the Qur'ān. Muslims all over the world know both names and use them when they send blessings of God on his soul.

What impact do you think the loss of his parents had on the early life and character of Muhammad (pbuh)? At the end of this chapter, check your answer.

HIS CHILDHOOD

The early life of Muhammad (pbuh) was eventful, as the following two incidents illustrate.

A Miracle Cleansing of the Heart

A few days after his birth, Muhammad (pbuh) was given to a foster mother, Halima, who brought him up in her village home. It was an Arab custom in those days to let babies of good families be reared by a foster mother. Amina entrusted Muhammad (pbuh) to Halima, who brought him back to his mother after fostering him for two years. But after pleading with Amina, Halima took him back again. The main reason for doing this was that while this child was in Halima's house, her date trees, her sheep and her camel all thrived and Halima lived happily.

After Halima took him back from his mother, a strange miracle happened. One day the child was playing in the fields, when all of a sudden he saw two people coming towards him. One held him tightly. The other cut his chest with a sharp knife, brought out some black bile from his heart, cleaned it, put his heart back and sewed up his chest. When they were gone, Muhammad (pbuh) got up, shaken – but he was quite normal. Was it a vision or reality? Many Muslim sages explain that this is how God cured Muhammad (pbuh) of the vile element in human nature.

Halima's daughter saw what was happening and ran to tell Halima. When Halima heard from Muhammad (pbuh) all that had taken place, she was afraid and returned him to Amina.

The Miracle of the Cloud and Bahira

The incident took place when Muhammad (pbuh) was a boy of 12. His uncle Abu Talib, who took care of him after the death of his grandfather, was going to Syria in connection with business. Because Muhammad (pbuh) liked always to be with his uncle, Abu Talib took him on the journey. Their trade caravan halted in an oasis near Basra, where a Christian monk named Bahira had a monastery. Bahira saw a low cloud between the sun and the travellers, hovering over the oasis where the Arab caravan halted. He had a manuscript which predicted the coming of the last prophet, and it described his features. Bahira invited the traders to eat with him. They left Muhammad (pbuh) with the animals and the goods. Bahira saw the cloud giving shade to the place where Muhammad (pbuh) was. He asked the traders if they had left anyone with the caravan, and after learning that a young boy was there he requested them to call him. After the meal Bahira talked to Abu Talib and Muhammad (pbuh). Abu Talib wanted to pose as Muhammad's (pbuh) father, perhaps to protect him, but Bahira knew from the manuscript that he was an orphan. When Abu Talib admitted that he was Muhammad's (pbuh) uncle, Bahira told him: 'He is the last prophet. Take your brother's son back to his country. Guard him against the enemies. By God, if they see him and know of him that which I know, they will try to do him harm. Great things are in store for your brother's son.' The monk then kissed the 'Seal' of the Last Prophet, a swollen area on the back of Muhammad's (pbuh) shoulder. When someone asked Bahira how he knew all this, he said, 'I saw the trees and stones bowing down to him and the cloud giving shade.'

Muhammad's (pbuh) faith in God

Bahira also wanted to know about his way of living, and asked him to swear by al-Lāt and al-'Uzza. Muhammad (pbuh) replied that he would not swear, for he did not believe in these idols. When Bahira then asked him to swear in the name of Allah, he agreed.

1   What were the two names of the Prophet? Who gave him those names?
2   What signs of future greatness can be found in the early life of Muhammad (pbuh)?
3   What evidence is there for believing that young Muhammad (pbuh) was a monotheist (someone who believes in only one God) from childhood?
4   Who was Bahira? What made him believe that young Muhammad (pbuh) was going to be the last prophet?

HIS YOUTH

'Al-Amīn' – the Trustworthy

Muhammad (pbuh) grew up as a quiet, lovable youth. He came to be known as a truthful, trustworthy young man. People believed that he would never betray any trust or break any promise. Someone once asked him to wait at a particular place where he would meet him. That person forgot, but Muhammad (pbuh) never left the place. After many hours the man remembered, went there and found Muhammad (pbuh) still waiting for him. This illustrates how Muhammad (pbuh) never broke his word, however difficult it might turn out to be to fulfil his commitment. This was why people would call him 'al-Amīn' – the Trustworthy.

Social Service

Muhammad's (pbuh) heart was always pained to see the corruption and cruelty in his country. He helped to form a confederacy among Makkan tribes, especially with some influential young people. Their duty was to find ways and means of stopping violence and preserving and maintaining peace, of seeing that justice was done and injustice not done, of upholding the right of the weak, the poor and the destitute, and of helping strangers and travellers who were often cheated and looted. This he succeeded in doing after people had decided to end the long war between the Quraysh and the neighbouring Qais tribe. This war was known as the Battle of Fijar. A peace committee was formed under an agreement known as the Agreement of Fudul, the place where the agreement was made.

HIS MATURITY

Marriage with Khadijah

Khadijah was a rich widow of high social status in Makkah. When she first came to know of Muhammad (pbuh) and of his truthfulness and honesty, she appointed him to trade for her. This he did very well. Khadijah sent her slave Maisarah as an assistant to Muhammad (pbuh). The profit from the trade went far beyond Khadijah's expectations, and the slave Maisarah also reported to her on Muhammad's honesty and fair dealings. This convinced her of his greatness. She sent a proposal of marriage to him. Muhammad (pbuh) referred the matter to his uncle, who was delighted, and the marriage took place, even though Khadijah was 40 and Muhammad (pbuh) was only 25.

Khadijah gave her husband total charge of her business, and he did not marry again as long as she was alive. Even though he had other wives later on, his love for Khadijah was foremost in his heart, a love that always made his second wife, Ayesha, jealous. Khadijah was the mother of all Muhammad's (pbuh) children except one, Ibrahim, born of Maria, a slave girl sent to him from the King of Ethiopia when he was in Medina. Sadly, only one daughter by Khadijah, Fatima, was still alive when he died. As his eldest son was called Qasim, Muhammad (pbuh) came to be called 'Abul Qasim' – father of Qasim.

Vision of a Society Freed from Slavery

Muhammad (pbuh) hated the way slaves were treated, but it was only after marrying Khadijah that he was able to buy and set some of them free. Khadijah had given him a young slave, Zaid, as a gift. Zaid had been stolen from home by someone who sold him to a Makkan who gave him to Khadijah. When Zaid's father learnt where his son was, he came to claim him. Muhammad (pbuh) then told Zaid that he was free to go with his father, but Zaid had become so attached to him that he refused to go. Muhammad (pbuh) declared that from that time on he would regard Zaid as his own son. This illustrates Muhammad's (pbuh) way of treating slaves as his equals.

Illiteracy

Muhammad (pbuh) was illiterate. He did not receive any formal schooling, and did not even know the Arabic alphabet. Before his marriage he was poor, and worked as a shepherd. Later on he was occupied with his trade, family life and meditation (see below). As a result he never learnt how to read or write. This fact is regarded by Muslims as evidence that the revelations in the Qur'ān are God-given and not made up by Muhammad (pbuh).

Seclusion and Meditation for 15 Years

A period of seclusion and meditation in a cave in Mount Hira near Makkah was the most decisive part of Muhammad's (pbuh) life so far. Khadijah gave him wholehearted support. She was convinced of his great mission, and so she never objected to this retreat. She continued to support what he was doing, even though she was worried about his safety when he went into the cave for several days at a time taking only some dried bread, dates and water. Neither she nor their daughter Fatima disclosed this secret to anyone. It was carefully guarded. He would generally be away for a day or two. The longest time was 15 days. Very few details of his experiences at this time are known to us, although we know of the greetings that he would often hear: 'Peace be on you, O Messenger of God.' He would turn and look for the speaker, but could see no one.

Cave in Mount Hira

This sort of retreat would not have seemed strange to his tribe because it was a traditional practice among the descendants of Isma'il. In each generation there would be one or two such people. From what Muhammad (pbuh) said about it later, it appears that at first he had good dreams, and then visions about the Unseen; then his eyesight was transformed and he saw with his physical eyes the angel Gabriel and other angels. This encounter is described in more detail in Chapter 3.

His Wisdom

Muhammad (pbuh) was becoming a person to whom the people of Makkah brought their disputes. He was seen to be an honest, fair judge who always tried to give truthful answers. Sometimes, as we have seen, he was called 'al-Amīn', the trustworthy one. The following story shows his skills at work.

The wisdom of Muhammad (pbuh)

Within this period of meditation, one significant incident took place, which indicated people's trust in Muhammad (pbuh) and his wisdom. When he was 35 years old, the Ka'ba, the house of God that Abraham and Isma'il had rebuilt, suffered from torrential rain, and later flood. The tribal leaders dismantled the house, rebuilt it and covered it with a wooden roof. Trouble started when they were about to replace the black stone which had been fixed by Abraham and Isma'il at one of the corners. This stone was always regarded with reverence. The practice of all visitors to the Ka'ba was to kiss the stone and then to walk round the building.

The question arose as to who should put the stone back in its place. Discussion led to arguments among tribal leaders, and almost to bloodshed. When they saw Muhammad (pbuh) entering the arena, they decided unanimously to make him their arbitrator. Muhammad (pbuh) accepted this invitation. He spread his cloak on the ground, and placed the black stone on it. Then he requested all the tribal leaders to hold the edges of the mantle and carry the stone to the Ka'ba. This they did. Then Muhammad (pbuh) raised the stone and placed it in the corner where it was supposed to be. Everyone was satisfied, and bloodshed was avoided.

We can see the kind of person that God chose to send his message to. But when Muhammad (pbuh) began preaching it, the same people who had trusted and respected him turned against him. In the next chapter we shall look at these conflicts, and at Muhammad's (pbuh) obedience to God's instructions to preach and suffer with patience and never to yield.

?

1 **a** What qualities in the young Muhammad's (pbuh) personality might his friends value most?

b Some people neglected Muhammad (pbuh) because he was poor and an orphan. What qualities were even they forced to respect?

2 Some people say that Muhammad (pbuh) made up the Qur'ān by learning about religion and other revealed books from the Jews and Christians that he met on his business trips. Why do Muslims reject that idea and believe that the Qur'ān came directly from God? Are there some characteristics of Muhammad (pbuh), which can be put forward in support of the Muslim view?

<table>
<tr><td>

Chapter

3

</td><td>

The Prophet Starts Preaching

</td></tr>
</table>

THE FIRST REVELATIONS: *WAHY*

One day, during the frequent visits of Muhammad (pbuh) to the cave in Mount Hira near Makkah, a strange incident occurred. He was 40 years old at the time. In the cave he saw someone with a human form who told him, 'Read!' and Muhammad (pbuh) said, 'I cannot read.' The person embraced him and said again, 'Read!' and he repeated, 'I cannot read.' Again the being pressed Muhammad (pbuh) to him almost to the limit of his endurance and repeated, 'Read!' Muhammad (pbuh) again replied, 'I cannot read.' Then the being pressed him a third time, and said:

إِقْرَأْ بِاسْمِ رَبِّكَ الَّذِىْ خَلَقَ ۟

خَلَقَ الْإِنْسَانَ مِنْ عَلَقٍ ۟

إِقْرَأْ وَ رَبُّكَ الْأَكْرَمُ ۟

الَّذِىْ عَلَّمَ بِالْقَلَمِ ۟

عَلَّمَ الْإِنْسَانَ مَا لَمْ يَعْلَمْ ۟

Recite: In the Name of your Lord who created, created Man of a blood-clot.
Recite: And your Lord is the Most Generous who taught by the Pen,
taught Man that he knew not.

Qur'ān, 96:1–5

Muhammad (pbuh) said later that when the being had left him, he felt as though the words he recited had been written on his heart. Ideas raced through his mind: 'Was it an evil spirit? Am I possessed? Have I become a poet?' Muhammad (pbuh) fled from the cave and started rushing down the hill. He heard a voice, 'O Muhammad, you are the messenger of God, and I am the angel Gabriel.' He looked up and saw the angel. Whichever way he turned he saw the angel in front of him. He rushed back home shivering. Khadijah asked him what was wrong, and he told her what had happened. Khadijah assured him, 'You are definitely the Prophet, it was surely an angel and not an evil spirit.'

Khadijah then went to her cousin Waraqa bin Nawfal, a Christian *Hanīf* who did not believe in idol worship. He listened to everything that Khadijah told him and assured her that she was right.

Mount Hira (Jabal Noor), where the first revelation came to the Prophet

13

The next morning Muhammad (pbuh) told Waraqa about the whole incident. Waraqa said, 'You are the Prophet about whom prophecy has been made. The angel that you saw is the same angel who brought messages to other prophets. You will be persecuted and you will have to leave this place. Evil people will drive you out. If I am alive when you are asked to preach I shall accept you and follow you.' But Waraqa died a few days later before Prophet Muhammad (pbuh) started preaching.

After this assurance from Waraqa, the Prophet was calm and confident. When messages started coming, he was able to receive them without any hesitation. But it was not an easy experience – he would go almost into a trance. Following his instructions, his companions would cover him with a sheet or blanket. Even during the middle of winter he would get up exhausted, with perspiration all over his face and body. Then he would recite to his companions the verses revealed to him. These companions were the first Muslims, after Khadijah.

Writing Down and Memorising the Revelations

Prophet Muhammad (pbuh) later instructed some of his companions to write down the revelations, and some of them who had excellent memories to learn them by heart. Someone who memorises the Qur'ān is known as a *hāfiz* (pl. *huffāz*). Muhammad (pbuh) also received instructions through Gabriel as to the order in which the verses should be placed.

How the Revelations Came

The Prophet mentioned two ways in which the revelations came to him:

> Sometimes it comes to me like the reverberations of a bell, and that is the hardest upon me; the reverberations abate when I am awake and I am aware of the message. Sometimes the Angel takes the form of a man and speaks to me and I remember exactly what he says.
>
> Bukhārī

Muhammad (pbuh) Learns How To Pray

The angel Gabriel also taught Muhammad (pbuh) how to perform ritual ablution (*wudū*) to purify himself, and how to pray in all the postures: standing, bowing, prostrating and sitting. He taught him the repeated utterances proclaiming God's Glory: *Allāhu Akbar* (God is most Great) and the final greeting *Assalāmu 'alaikum* (Peace be on you). The Prophet then taught Khadijah, and they prayed together. Muslims have prayed in this way ever since.

DIRECTION FROM GOD TO PREACH

After the first messages there was a period of silence, which made the Prophet worried. Then came the assurance that God had not forsaken him, and he was directed to 'declare your Lord's blessing' (Qur'ān, 93:11).

Only then did he start preaching, first to his own household, then among his nearest relations and then among those he knew. Khadijah was the first person to accept the Prophet's message, the first Muslim.

The Prophet's Early Preaching

After Khadijah and their daughter Fatima became Muslims, Ali (the Prophet's cousin) and Zaid (the young slave) accepted Islam too. Ali was the son of Abu Talib, and he was ten years old at the time. Muhammad (pbuh) had looked after Ali after his marriage to Khadijah.

Abu Bakr, a wise and wealthy businessman, became convinced of the truth of Islam when he talked to the Prophet, and he became the first adult male Muslim. He then persuaded a few others to accept Islam. Thus Talha, Uthman and Abdullah Ibn Masud joined the ranks of the Prophet's close companions. Umm Aiman was the first slave girl to become a Muslim. They all used to pray together in secrecy and greet each other with the greeting that the angel Gabriel had taught the Prophet – *Assalāmu 'alaikum* (Peace be on you).

The Prophet's companions
All those who accepted Islam and who tried to stay with the Prophet and follow him wholeheartedly became known as the Prophet's companions (*sahābah*, pl. *ashāb*). The best known were Khadijah, Fatima, Zaid, Ali, Abu Bakr, Talha, Uthman, Abdullah Ibn Masud, Umm Aiman and Bilal.

Why do you think Muslims prefer to call the men and women who came to believe the message which Muhammad (pbuh) preached his 'companions' rather than his 'followers'?

Public Preaching and Early Persecution

Sermon on Mount Safa

Within two years the order came from God for Muhammad (pbuh) to preach openly. The first thing he did was to call everyone to Mount Safa near the Ka'ba.

Muhammad (pbuh) climbed the hill and loudly called the Quraysh to assemble. When they came he said, 'If I tell you that a big army is coming to attack you from the other side, will you believe me?' All of them said, 'Of course. We all know and believe that you always speak the truth.'

Then he said, 'I then ask you to pray to Allah alone. Give up worshipping idols. Give up evil ways. Then you will be successful. If you don't then you will suffer badly, and it will be too late to do anything to save yourself.'

Most of those assembled did not know what to say. But some were angry and shouted, 'You have gone mad.' Abu Lahab, one of the Prophet's uncles, shouted, 'May Allah destroy you. Have you called us for this?' He then left and all the others went away.

Preaching to his Near Relations

A few days after the sermon on Mount Safa, the Prophet invited his uncles, cousins and nephews to his house. He said, 'I have given you a great religion. Whoever follows it will have success in this world and in the hereafter. Is there anyone who wants to help me in this mission?' Only young Ali got up and said that he would. Abu Lahab, the Prophet's uncle, again got angry and walked out. Others kept quiet and silently went away.

SUFFERING AND PERSECUTION

The First Martyr

The number of Muslims reached 40. Prophet Muhammad (pbuh) went to the Ka'ba and proclaimed that God is One and that he was God's Prophet, and he then invited everyone to follow the truth and give up idol worshipping. This was regarded by the non-believers in Islam as the biggest insult to their faith and customs. They attacked the Prophet. Harith bin Hala, a new Muslim, rushed out of his house to protect the Prophet. He was killed, and so became the first martyr in the history of Islam.

No Compromise with Falsehood

The leaders of the Quraysh tribe wanted a compromise with Muhammad (pbuh). They saw that he was in single-minded pursuit of what God had asked him to do. At first they ignored him, thinking that he was possessed. But then they found him openly proclaiming his faith, and they discovered that some important influential people were flocking to him. And so they offered him leadership, wealth and the most beautiful woman of Arabia if only he would stop preaching against their gods and goddesses and their way of life. Muhammad's (pbuh) only powerful support, his uncle Abu Talib, was himself wavering. But the Prophet told his uncle, 'Even if they give me the sun in one hand and the moon in the other, I shall not give up what God has asked me to do.' This convinced Abu Talib of Muhammad's (pbuh) total commitment and so he told Muhammad (pbuh) that he would support him. This he did, until his death in the tenth year of the Prophet's mission.

Discuss why Muhammad (pbuh) felt it would be wrong to compromise with those who would not accept his message.

God Teaches Patience

As more and more influential people of different tribes started accepting Islam, the Makkan unbelievers, especially their leaders, of whom Abu Jahl was the most outspoken, increased their taunts and tortures. It was the slaves who suffered most. Bilal, a black slave, who later became a great companion of the Prophet, was forced to lie naked on hot sand with heavy stones on his chest. He cried only 'Allah the One, Allah the One', and would have died if Abu Bakr had not bought him from his cruel master and freed him. Other slaves were also tortured. Even women slaves were made to suffer. But they did not give up their faith, nor did their faith weaken. God gave them strength to remain patient.

MIGRATION TO ABYSSINIA

When the torture became almost unbearable and the unbelievers were ready to kill the Muslims and take away their property, the Prophet allowed a group of Muslims to migrate to Abyssinia to seek protection. This migration took place in *Rajab*, the seventh month in the lunar calendar, in the fifth year of the Prophet's mission.

Those who emigrated to Abyssinia were pursued by the Quraysh. The Quraysh asked the Abyssinian king, Negus, to hand the Muslims over to them because, they said, they were rebels. King Negus wanted to hear the Muslims' story. This is what Ja'far, the Prophet's cousin, a son of Abu Talib, told the king:

> We were a people steeped in ignorance and immorality, worshipping idols and committing all sorts of evil and injustice, and treating guests badly. The strong among us would exploit the weak. Then God sent a Prophet from among us. We knew his lineage, truthfulness, trustworthiness and integrity. He called us to worship God alone, testify to His Oneness, and give up worshipping the stones and idols that our ancestors used to worship. He commanded us to speak the truth, honour our promises, respect the ties of kinship, be good to our neighbours, abstain from crimes and bloodshed, and avoid adultery and fornication. He has commanded us not to bear false witness, nor to appropriate an orphan's property or falsely accuse a married woman. So we worship God only, follow Him in what He has told us is lawful, and avoid what He has forbidden us to do. That is why our people have attacked us, treated us harshly and tried to make us give up our religion and our worship of God, and take us back to immorality and the worship of idols. That is why we seek your protection, so that we may live in justice and peace.

The king listened and asked the Muslims to recite a revelation. Ja'far recited verses from *Sūrah Maryam* (Chapter 'Mary'), which spoke of the birth of Christ. King Negus and the bishops wept. Then King Negus said, 'This has definitely come from the same source as the message that Jesus brought.'

King Negus then turned to the Quraysh and said to them, 'You may go. By God, I will not hand them over to you; they shall not be betrayed.'

CONVERSIONS TO ISLAM

The two most powerful opponents of Islam at this time were Abu Jahl and 'Umar. Muhammad (pbuh) used to pray to God to convert them. God informed Muhammad (pbuh), through the angel Gabriel, that He had accepted his prayer partially, and had granted faith to 'Umar. The Prophet received this message on the day 'Umar left his house with a naked sword to kill him. This is what happened:

The Conversion of 'Umar

On the way to the Prophet's house, 'Umar met someone who had secretly become a Muslim. When this person heard that 'Umar was out to kill the Prophet, he told him that 'Umar's own sister and brother-in-law had accepted Islam. 'Umar then rushed to his sister's house. There, Khabbab, one of the Prophet's companions, was reading some verses of the Qur'ān with them.

When 'Umar called out to his brother-in-law, they put away the page of the Qur'ān, and the companion hid himself behind a screen. 'Umar was full of rage. He asked his sister and brother-in-law whether they had become Muslims. When they said yes, he started beating his brother-in-law. 'Umar's sister tried to save her husband, but a blow hit her and blood gushed out. This stopped 'Umar. Suddenly something happened to him. He asked to see what they were hiding.

'Umar's sister told him defiantly, 'You are unclean, I won't give it to you.'

They were surprised when 'Umar asked, 'Can I be purified?' It seemed that 'Umar was sincere, and so his sister taught him how to perform the ablution, and he did so.

The page that was given to 'Umar to read contained the opening verses of *Sūrah Tā-Hā* (a chapter in the Qur'ān). The moment 'Umar read it he said, 'How beautiful and noble are these words.' The companion, Khabbab, came out from behind the screen when he heard this and said to 'Umar, ''Umar, I have hope that God has chosen you through the prayer of His Prophet.' 'O Khabbab,' replied 'Umar, 'Where will Muhammad (pbuh) be now, that I may go to him and enter Islam?'

Khabbab took him to the Prophet's house. Though the companions were afraid, the Prophet instructed them to open the door. 'O Messenger of God,' 'Umar said, 'I have come to you that I may declare my faith in God, and in His Messenger and what he has brought forth from God.'

'*Allāhu Akbar* (God is Most Great),' said the Prophet in such a way that everyone realised that 'Umar had entered Islam.

The conversion of 'Umar took place in the sixth year of the Prophet's mission.

The Conversion of Hamzah

The next most influential person to accept Islam in the same year was the great warrior, Hamzah, one of the Prophet's uncles. Hamzah had gone out hunting, and when he returned a woman told him that Abu Jahl had taunted Muhammad (pbuh) and hit him.

As Muhammad (pbuh) was under the protection of his family, Hamzah felt insulted. He rushed to the Ka'ba, and found Abu Jahl sitting by Mount Safa talking to his followers. Hamzah took his bow and hit Abu Jahl hard and then said, 'Now know that I also accept Islam and shall support Muhammad (pbuh) wholeheartedly. Be careful.'

Abu Jahl's followers wanted to fight. But Abu Jahl stopped them and told them that Hamzah had hit him because he had hit Muhammad (pbuh).

FURTHER SUFFERING

First Collective Prayer at the Ka'ba

It was after the conversion of 'Umar that the Prophet persuaded all the new Muslims to go to the house of God, the Ka'ba, and say their prayers openly. The unbelievers saw this as an open defiance of their gods and goddesses and they boycotted the Hashimite clan of the Prophet, making the Muslims suffer.

The Boycott

After some of the Muslims had emigrated to Abyssinia, Abu Jahl succeeded in persuading other tribal chiefs to boycott the family of Hashim, a supporter of the Prophet, and confine them in a mountain pass that is now called Shibi Abu Talib.

The boycott continued for three years. Secretly many people supported the family and brought them food to prevent them from dying of starvation. Eventually the boycott had to be called off, as serious differences began to arise between the people who supported the Hashimites and those who didn't.

The Prophet, the Hashimite clan and the other believers did not take recourse to fighting. They obeyed God's commands, 'And bear patiently what they say, and forsake them graciously' (Qur'ān, 73:10) and 'Give respite to the unbelievers; delay with them awhile' (Qur'ān, 86:17).

Deaths of Abu Talib and Khadijah

After the boycott ended, the two greatest supporters of the Prophet, Abu Talib and the Prophet's beloved wife Khadijah, died. Muhammad (pbuh) called this tenth year of his mission 'The Year of Sorrow'.

Suffering at Taif

After the deaths of Abu Talib and Khadijah, the situation in Makkah changed for the worse. The Prophet went to Taif (see the map on p. 5) to preach, thinking that his relations would protect him, but instead they set upon him. Young men and children started stoning him. It is reported that when he began to bleed, the angel Gabriel came to him and asked his permission to punish the wrongdoers by bringing the hills together and crushing them. The Prophet replied, 'God has sent me as a mercy to mankind. Though these people may not believe, their children may,' and he then took shelter in a vineyard. A slave who gave him water and listened to him in the vineyard became a Muslim.

THE PROPHET'S BODILY ASCENT (MI'RĀJ) TO THE THRONE OF GOD

God had destined for Muhammad (pbuh) glory and success in a new place where he would have to go. This turned out to be Medina. But before that journey a miraculous event took place that gave him unbounded energy, removed from his mind all the pain and shock of the deaths of Abu Talib and Khadijah, and of his suffering at Taif. What took place is a central event in Muhammad's (pbuh) life. It is also central to Islam. It showed the Prophet and his companions the highest reward and supreme pleasure that a human being could get during his or her life on earth. This miraculous event was *al-mi'rāj*, the bodily ascent of Muhammad (pbuh) to the throne of God, his meeting with God and the gifts of God for him and for all Muslims. The Prophet was taken by Gabriel on an animal like a horse with wings, a *burāq*, to Jerusalem, where he met other prophets and acted as their *imām* (leader in prayer).

The angel Gabriel then gave the Prophet three glasses of drink to choose from, one containing water, one containing milk, and the other containing wine. The Prophet chose the milk. The angel Gabriel appreciated his choice, and said that the Prophet's religion would remain the natural religion (*dīn al-fitrah*), or the religion that is natural to humanity.

The Dome of the Rock, Jerusalem. The mosque was built between 688 and 692 CE.

The angel Gabriel then took him up to the seven skies to visit Hell and Heaven and meet most of the important prophets, from Adam to Abraham (peace be upon them all). Then Muhammad (pbuh) went beyond the seventh sky to the throne of God, where Gabriel did not dare to go.

The Significance of this Ascent for Muslims

The significance of the Prophet's ascent is spiritual. Muhammad (pbuh) had submitted totally to God, so God's grace descended upon him and led him to a state of great spiritual consciousness.

The relevance of this experience for Muslims as a whole lies in the instructions which the Prophet was given about the daily prayers. God told him that it was His Will that human beings should pray five times a day. In this way they too could receive God's grace and enter a state of spiritual consciousness.

This instruction from God to pray five times a day resulted in *salāh* (prayer) becoming the central pillar of Islam. Through *salāh*, a human being can reach nearness to God. That is why the Prophet said, 'Salāh is ascension (*mi'rāj*) for a faithful person.'

?

1   Imagine that you had been with Muhammad (pbuh) during the events described in this chapter. Write a letter to a friend in Jerusalem giving your impressions.

2   Try to explain why some people refused to believe that Muhammad (pbuh) was a prophet. When you have written down your reasons, discuss them with a Muslim.

3   **a**   What is an idol?
    b   Why did Muhammad (pbuh) attack idolatry?

4   What was the importance of Khadijah in the early years of Muhammad's (pbuh) ministry?

5   Muhammad (pbuh) said that if he had told people of an advancing army they would have believed him, but when he told them about the One God they did not. Imagine you were present. Discuss his words in a group (a) taking the part of those who did believe and (b) using the kinds of arguments of those who did not.

<table>
<tr>
<td>

Chapter
4

</td>
<td>

Hijrah and the First Islamic State

</td>
</tr>
</table>

HIJRAH-MIGRATION TO MEDINA

The Prophet's suffering and patience had reached their maximum limits. Muhammad (pbuh) received an instruction from God to leave Makkah. The opportunity came during the month of pilgrimage. It was the Prophet's habit to invite the pilgrims who came to Makkah during this period to accept the true path.

In 620 CE, six leading members of the Khazraz tribe of Medina became Muslim. The next year, five of these and seven other leading members came for *hajj* (pilgrimage), and entered into an agreement with Muhammad (pbuh). They agreed to obey none but Allah, not to steal, commit adultery, kill children or disobey him. This agreement was made at a place near Makkah known as 'Aqaba, and the agreement came to be known as the First Covenant of Al-'Aqaba. The Prophet sent one of his companions, Musa bin 'Umair, to teach them the Qur'ān and give them religious instruction.

The Prophet then prepared to go to Medina. He discussed this with his uncle Abbas who joined him the following year at 'Aqaba where they held a secret meeting with members of the Khazraz tribe and some of the Aws tribe. They pledged to take Muhammad (pbuh) and protect him. Then they asked, 'Tell us O Prophet of Allah, what will be our reward if we remain true to our oath?' The Prophet said, 'Paradise'. Then one by one they took hold of his outstretched hand and promised to protect him. The Prophet had already promised never to leave them.

After this the Prophet instructed other Muslims to emigrate to Medina. In 622 CE the Makkan unbelievers plotted to kill the Prophet. But the Prophet asked Ali to sleep in his place in his bed, and the Prophet and Abu Bakr left for Medina without being seen. When the unbelievers realised that they had been fooled, they went in search of the Prophet and drew very near the cave in which he and Abu Bakr were hiding. But God saved them. A spider built a nest at the mouth of the cave, and a bird laid eggs in a corner. When the unbelievers saw this they went elsewhere. After three nights the Prophet set out again towards Medina and reached Quba. There he built the first mosque.

Finally, in September, 622 CE, or *Rabī' al-Awwal,* 1 AH, in the thirteenth year of his active life as a prophet, Muhammad (pbuh) and Abu Bakr entered the city of Medina. The Prophet was received with great honour and jubilation.

It is this Hijrah (migration) of the Prophet that became the starting point of the Muslim Hijrī calendar.

The Islamic Calendar (Hijrī Calendar)

Although the Arabs followed the lunar months, they had no fixed year to begin their calendar. They referred to 'Noah's flood' or to Abraham as reference points in time. After discussion, the year of Prophet Muhammad's (pbuh) entry into Medina was chosen to be the first Hijrī year, and the calendar came to be called the Hijrī calendar. *Muharram* was selected to be the first month of the lunar year. The calendar thus began from the first of *Muharram* of the first year of Hijrī, or 16 July, 622 CE.

The lunar months vary from 29 to 30 days and begin with the new moon. A Hijrī year is 11 days shorter than a solar year in the Gregorian calendar. Leap years are not used. Hijrī months do not therefore follow the seasons and an elaborate system has to be used to find a corresponding Hijrī date in the Gregorian calendar.

The Hijrī calendar months and some religiously important dates are listed below:

Muharram	10th: *Āshūrā'*
Safar	
Rabī' al-Awwal	12th: *Mīlād al-Nabī*
Rabī' al-Thānī	
Jamādī al-Awwal	
Jamādī al-Thānī	
Rajab	27th: *Lailat al-Mi'rāj*
Sha'bān	15th: *Lailat al-Barāt*
Ramadān	month of fasting; *Lailat al-Qadr*
Shawwāl	*'Īd al-Fitr* festival, also known as *Bairam* or *'Īd-Ramadān* or *'Īd al-Saghīr* (the small festival)
Zulqa'da	
Dhul Hijja	month for pilgrimage (*hajj*). 10th: *'Īd al-Adhā* (festival of sacrifice) or *'Īd al-Kabīr* (the great festival).

The year 2000 CE will be 1421 AH (Anno Hijrī).

THE PROPHET IN MEDINA

When the Prophet first arrived in Medina, he allowed his camel, called Qaswā', to stop where it wanted. The camel stopped and the Prophet got down. He later bought that plot of land and constructed the mosque which is still known as the Prophet's mosque (*al-Masjid al-Nabawī*). He also built two thatched rooms by the side of the mosque, one for his wife Sawdah, who was a widow when he married her, and the other for Ayesha, daughter of Abu Bakr, who was betrothed to him.

A New Brotherhood

Immediately after his arrival in Medina, the Prophet did two things which set the whole pattern for the future of Islam and the Muslims. The first was the establishment of a perfect brotherhood between those who had emigrated from Makkah (the *Muhājirūn*) and the helpers of Medina (the *Ansār*). He arranged, with the wholehearted consent of the Medinite Muslims, that each one of them should take one of the emigrants from Makkah and share with him his property and his life. Many Makkans accepted this generous offer on condition that they would take money only as a loan. This shelter for the emigrants formed an important bond

The Prophet's mosque in Medina in the past (left) and today (right)

which laid the foundations of Muslim brotherhood, and set a noble example for Muslims for all ages. It also saved the new community from any potential rivalries, and set the standard for the future Muslim community (*ummah*) (see Chapters 8 and 17).

The City State of Medina

The other thing the Prophet did was to establish the nucleus of a Muslim state in the city of Medina. Along with the Muslim tribes, the Jewish tribes and others who worshipped many gods also accepted him as head of the state. The Prophet dictated the charter which became the first constitution of the state. It is generally known as the Charter (or Pact or Covenant) of Medina.

The Jews were very powerful in Medina. They were traders, merchants and usurers, and they controlled the economic life of the pagan tribes. The Pact amounted to an agreement for peaceful coexistence, an alliance for cooperation against aggression and freedom for each community to practise its own religion. Some of the terms of this Pact were as follows:

- The Muslims and the Jews shall live together as one people.

- Neither of the two parties shall interfere with the faith of the other.

- If a third party attacks, each of the parties shall be bound to help one another in the event of war.

- If Medina is attacked, both parties shall join hands to defend it.

- Both parties shall regard Medina as a sacred place, and bloodshed shall be forbidden there.

- The Prophet shall be the final court of appeal in the event of a dispute.

Thus a state with Muslim and non-Muslim people became the ideal model of a state for all Muslims. It had God as the sovereign, and the Prophet as the law-giver, guide and executor. The Muslims had found a centre, a law-giver and a judge. Tribal laws were replaced by the basic principle of justice – irrespective of caste, creed or colour. The absolute moral principles which Ja'far spoke of to the Abyssinian king (see Chapter 3) could now become the basis not only for individual personal improvement, but also for the legal principles and rules of society.

The new society had to be organised, disciplined, integrated and saved from the schemes of its opponents. Because of these new needs, new revelations started coming to the Prophet.

NEW DIRECTION FOR PRAYER (*QIBLAH*)

In the second Hijrī year, Muhammad (pbuh) received a revelation that Muslims should face the Ka'ba at Makkah whenever they prayed. Until then they had prayed towards the Temple in Jerusalem. Since the Ka'ba was originally built by Adam for the worship of Allah, and was later rebuilt by Abraham, this change meant that Muslims now identified themselves with the ancient religious tradition of Adam and Eve, Abraham and Isma'il. The direction Muslims face when they pray is known as the *qiblah*.

New Importance of Makkah

Makkah now occupied a more important place in the hearts of all new Muslims, not only the emigrants. The city was to be treated from now on not just as the birth place of the Prophet, or a place having a house of God, but as a place of convergence for all Muslims. It became the central place for Islam, the holiest of holy places, the holy sanctuary for all Muslims for all ages.

CALL FOR PRAYER (*ADHĀN*)

After the *mi'rāj* (ascension) of Muhammad (pbuh) (see Chapter 3), it became obligatory for all Muslims to pray five times a day. When they came to Medina, the Muslims gathered to find out the times for prayer.

One night a companion of the Prophet met someone in a dream who taught him the call for prayer (*adhān*) which Muslims know today. He reported his dream to the Prophet, who said, 'It is a genuine vision,' and told the companion to teach the call to Bilal, the black slave who suffered torture for his acceptance of Islam before he was freed by Abu Bakr. The first call to prayer was thus given by Bilal. The person who gives this call is known as *muadhdhin* (sometimes written as *muezzin*) and the call is known as *adhān*.

The Exact Wording of the *Adhān* as said by the Prophet

1   You must say:

God is most great (*Allāhu Akbar*)
God is most great (*Allāhu Akbar*)
God is most great (*Allāhu Akbar*)
God is most great (*Allāhu Akbar*)
raising your voice while saying the words.

2 Then you must say:

I testify that there is no god but God (*Ashhadu al-lā ilāha illa Allāh*)
I testify that there is no god but God (*Ashhadu al-lā ilāha illa Allāh*)

3 I testify that Muhammad is God's Messenger (*Ashhadu anna Muhammadar Rasū lullāh*)
I testify that Muhammad is God's Messenger (*Ashhadu anna Muhammadar Rasū lullāh*)

4 Come to prayer (*Hayya 'alā as-Salāh*)
Come to prayer (*Hayya 'alā as-Salāh*)

5 Come to salvation (*Hayya 'alā al-Falāh*)
Come to salvation (*Hayya 'alā al-Falāh*)

and if it is morning prayer then you must say in addition at this place:

Prayer is better than sleep (*Assalātu khairum min an-nawm*)
Prayer is better than sleep (*Assalātu khairum min an-nawm*)

6 God is most great (*Allāhu Akbar*)
God is most great (*Allāhu Akbar*)

7 There is no god but God (*Lā ilāha illa Allāh*)
There is no god but God (*Lā ilāha illa Allāh*)

After the *adhān*, Muslims are asked to stand in rows behind the prayer leader (*imām*).

SHARĪ'AH During the first three years of Hijrah, the Prophet received new revelations. These were orders to perform *sawm* (fasting) during the month of *Ramadān*, to give *zakāh* (money due to the poor), and to prohibit the charging of interest in all transactions. Wine drinking and gambling were also prohibited. Laws regarding marriage and divorce, the rights of married women, inheritance and orphans were also revealed to the Prophet.

All these messages came when the Prophet was facing situations for which he could find no solution in any of the messages that had already come to him. But though they came as solutions to particular problems, they were to serve as general rules for all time. They came as general principles to be applied to all such occasions or similar situations. These principles, and all other rules and regulations, form what is known as *Sharī'ah* or the Divine Law for humanity (see also Chapters 9 and 16).

?

1 Why do you think that Muhammad's (pbuh) first act on arriving in Medina was to build a mosque?

2 What were the political, social and legal effects of setting up the Medina State?

3 By following the lunar year in religious practices, Muslims in different parts of the world feel they are being treated with justice, especially in fasting during the month of *Ramadān*. Comment on this statement.

<table>
<tr><td>

Chapter 5

</td><td>

Jihād *and the Conquest of Makkah*

</td></tr>
</table>

THE BEGINNING OF JIHĀD

In Makkah all the revelations had told the Muslims to bear suffering with patience. But in Medina, a new message came. It was an order to save Islam because the Quraysh were now planning to attack the Muslims and to eliminate them. The only way to establish peace now was by conquering Makkah, the headquarters of the Quraysh tribe and the centre for the Muslims.

God's message came in the very first Hijrī year:

> Leave is given to those who fight because
> they were wronged – surely God is able
> to help them –
> who were expelled from their habitations
> without right, except that they say
> 'Our Lord is God.' Had God not driven back
> the people, some by the means of others,
> there had been destroyed cloisters and churches,
> oratories and mosques, wherein God's Name
> is much mentioned. Assuredly God will
> help him who helps Him – surely God is
> All-strong, All-mighty –
> who, if We establish them in the land,
> perform the prayer, and pay the alms,
> and bid to honour, and forbid dishonour;
> and unto God belongs the issue
> of all affairs.
>
> Qur'ān, 22:40–1

The Prophet made it clear that this permission to fight was granted only to preserve the Truth, not to extol oneself or one's party or one's country. And fighting is justified only when all other means of establishing peace have been exhausted.

The Qur'ān condemns bloodshed and war (Qur'ān, 2:11), but fighting in the cause of God is obligatory if the opponents of Islam start destroying God's order. That is why this verse was revealed in Medina:

> And fight in the way of God with those
> who fight with you, but aggress not: God loves
> not the aggressors.
>
> Qur'ān, 2:187

Even when the enemy wants to fight, the duty of Muslims is to invite them to peace. The Prophet told Mu'āz bin Jabal, the commander of the Muslim army:

Do not fight them before you call them [to submit to God or to a peace treaty]. And if they decline, do not fight them until they take the initiative, and when they do, wait until they slay your men. Then, show them the body of the slain and say to them, 'Is there no better way than this?' If God ordains that one single man from amongst them should submit to Him through your example it will be better for you than to own the whole world.

Bukhārī

Jihād means 'strife' or 'struggle'; that is using one's powers to the utmost against something which has earned God's disapproval. There are three kinds of objects of disapproval:

- a visible enemy,
- the devil,
- some defect in oneself.

Ultimately the purpose of *jihād* is for self-purification and the purification of human beings in society. The rest of this chapter describes the first *jihāds*, why and how they took place and what were the results. You will then understand how, from the practices of the Prophet and from God's messages, Islam wants Muslims to be ready to defend the Truth and to fight when attacked.

The Battle of Badr

After the Muslims emigrated to Medina, the Makkans seized their property and went to Damascus to trade with this wealth. As it was Muslim property that was being used by the Quraysh to trade, the Prophet decided to intervene and capture their goods. When he heard that Abu Sufyān, a Quraysh leader of Makkah, was returning from Syria, the Prophet himself and nearly all male Muslims came out to attack him. Abu Sufyān was alerted to the presence of the Medinite Muslims when date seeds were found in the camel dung at Badr, and he sent a message to Makkah for help. Abu Jahl, the other outstanding leader of the Quraysh, came out in support with a fully armed contingent of more than a thousand men. Abu Sufyān himself took a different route and returned safely to Makkah. But the Prophet and the Muslims got caught in Badr. They had only 313 men. But God granted them a victory. Most of the leading people of Makkah, including Abu Jahl, were killed and a large group of Makkans were captured. Included among the captured Makkans was Abbas, an uncle of the Prophet. He, and some others, accepted Islam but went back to Makkah. The rest had to be ransomed by the Makkans.

This decisive victory of a handful of Muslims convinced many tribes of God's help and of the prophethood of Muhammad (pbuh).

The Battle of Uhud

In retaliation for the defeat at Badr, the Quraysh brought an army of 3000 men and tried to enter Medina by force. That was how a battle took place on the mountain range of Uhud in the third Hijrī year. The Prophet placed a row of archers in defence, and instructed them never to leave their position. Khalid, who later became a great Muslim general, was then on the side of the Quraysh. He planned a ruse, feigning defeat and retreating to allow the Muslims to advance and loot. The archers were tempted by greed and they left their station. Khalid brought his men around behind the Muslims and attacked them, as they were now defenceless. Even the Prophet was hurt, and one of his teeth got broken, but the senior companions never left him. The Muslims managed to get together again and, joined by others, they rallied successfully and a defeat was averted. Then, in the afternoon, they retreated to higher ground, regrouped properly, and were able to attack again. The Makkans were not prepared to accept the high losses they would have to suffer if they tried to attack once more and they decided to retreat. The Prophet sent a contingent in pursuit to ensure that they did not return.

Many Muslims became martyrs at this battle, the most outstanding one being Hamzah, an uncle of the Prophet.

After the battle, God sent down revelations warning all the Muslims that this was a penalty from God for their disobedience of the Prophet in greedily searching for booty. This was thus a severe lesson for future guidance. The following verses were revealed after the battle as a warning:

> God has been true in His promise towards you
> when you blasted them by His leave; until
> you lost heart, and quarrelled about the matter,
> and were rebellious, after He had shown you
> that you longed for.
> Some of you there are that desire this world,
> and some of you there are desire the next world.
> Then He turned you from them, that He might try you;
> and He has pardoned you; and God is bounteous
> to the believers.

> Qur'ān, 3:145–7

? Imagine you are a Muslim who survived the battle of Uhud. Tell your family what happened and what moral lessons you learned from the experience.

The Battle of Ahzāb (the Battle of the Trenches)

The battle of Uhud was indecisive and it encouraged the unbelievers of Makkah to attack again. In the fifth Hijrī year, the Quraysh raised an army of 10 000 men and proceeded towards Medina.

The Quraysh army was supported by the Banu Nadīr, a Jewish tribe expelled from Medina when it was discovered that they had plotted to kill the Prophet, thus breaking the charter (see p. 23) and becoming an enemy. The Banu Nadīr moved from Medina to Khaiber and joined the Makkan Quraysh, assuring them of the assistance of other Medinite Jewish tribes.

On the advice of Salman al-Farsi, the only Persian companion of the Prophet, deep and wide trenches were dug around the whole of Medina. The Prophet himself helped to dig the trenches. Suddenly his axe hit an iron boulder and a flash of light seemed to spark. He dug again and there was another spark and a flash. The Prophet saw this as a sign that first the Persian Empire and then the Roman Empire

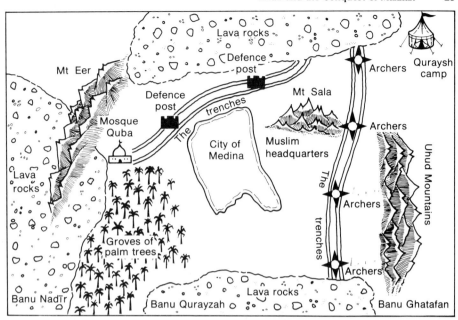

The Battle of the Trenches

would be defeated and conquered. He told his companions of this to give them strength, and informed them of the certainty of victory.

The deep and wide trenches surprised the enemy. They laid siege. Already they were in touch with the Banu Qurayzah, a Jewish tribe of Medina who, like Banu Nadīr, had tried to harm the Muslims. The Prophet sent a warning but they did not repent, nor did they stop their treacherous planning to help the Quraysh and attack the Muslims from behind. However, their attempts failed and the Quraysh lost food, help and morale.

Then the weather changed. Stormy winds, thunder and rain blew away the tents of the enemy, and they had to flee for their lives in a wild frenzy. The Muslims saw this as divine intervention.

After the war was over, the Banu Qurayzah were asked to choose an arbiter who would judge them for their secret betrayal at a moment of crisis. They chose Sa'd, the chief of the Aws, a tribe friendly to them. According to Sa'd's judgement, all male adults were beheaded.

The Treaty of Hudaibiyah

In the sixth Hijrī year, the Prophet had a dream that he was visiting the Ka'ba and walking round it. He decided to act according to his dream and visit the Ka'ba. With him went 1400 of his followers. When the Quraysh learned about this venture, they decided to stop the Prophet and his followers from entering Makkah. The Prophet and his followers were not fully armed, they had just their swords for personal protection. After intensive negotiations with the Prophet, the Quraysh leaders signed a treaty. As the Muslims had been waiting in Hudaibiyah outside Makkah, this treaty came to be known as the Treaty of Hudaibiyah.

The terms of the treaty were briefly as follows:

1 For the next ten years people were to enjoy peace and refrain from fighting each other.

2 There would be security of person and property of the Prophet's companions if they travelled to Makkah for *hajj* or *'umrah*, the pilgrimages, or for commerce on their way to Yemen or Taif, and the same security for the Quraysh if they went to Medina en route to Syria or Iraq for trade or commerce.

3 Anyone from Makkah going to the Prophet without the permission of the Quraysh would be handed over to the Quraysh, but anyone coming from Medina to Makkah would not be handed over to the Prophet.

4 Anyone who wanted to could become an ally of the Prophet or of the Quraysh.

5 There would be no violation of neutrality and no unfaithful action.

6 The Prophet and the Muslims were to withdraw that year and animals would be sacrificed outside the precincts of Makkah. The following year the Prophet and his companions would be allowed to enter Makkah and stay there for three nights, during which time the Quraysh would withdraw from their sight.

Most of the companions did not understand the implications of the treaty, but the Prophet insisted that everything was done under God's direction. That was why God had sent down a revelation saying, 'Surely We have given you a manifest victory' (Qur'ān, 48:1).

Though the third clause of the treaty seemed to be rather humiliating for the Muslims, it ultimately proved beneficial to them. Because of this clause, the Prophet had to send one person back to the Quraysh, but this person managed to kill his captors and he returned to the Prophet in Medina. The Prophet did not allow him to stay, however. That person, together with other new Muslims who could not join the Prophet in Medina, organised themselves outside Makkah, attacked Makkan caravans and carried on guerilla warfare against the Quraysh. As a result, the Makkan Quraysh themselves finally requested the Prophet to drop Clause 3 from the treaty.

The fourth and fifth clauses were also violated. Two years after the treaty had been signed, the Banu Bakr tribe (allies of the Quraysh) attacked the Banu Khuza'ah tribe (allies of the Prophet) while they were asleep. When they took refuge in the Ka'ba they were butchered in the sacred precincts. The Prophet immediately declared the Treaty of Hudaibiyah to be invalid.

Developments after the Treaty

During the two years of peace after the Treaty of Hudaibiyah, three important things happened:

● The Banu Nadīr (see p. 28) were attacked by the Prophet within two weeks of the signing of the Treaty of Hudaibiyah. The Prophet carried out the attack before they had had time to declare themselves allies of the Quraysh, and therefore immune from attack under the terms of the treaty. The Quraysh could not therefore come to the aid of the Banu Nadīr tribe. The Banu Nadīr were at this time living in Khaiber fortress, which was conquered by the Muslims after a hard struggle. Thus a vital centre for the enemies of Islam and the Muslims was destroyed.

● Two important members of the Makkan Quraysh, Khalid bin Walid, a great military genius who had been an invaluable asset to the Quraysh, and Amr Ibnul 'Ās, another Quraysh leader, were converted to Islam.

بسم الله الرّحمن الرّحيم
من محمّد بن عبد الله ورسوله الٰى
هرقل عظيم الرّوم سلام على من
اتبع الهدى امّا بعد فانّى ادعوك
بدعاية الاسلام اسلم تسلم يؤتك
الله اجرك مرّتين فان توليت فان
عليك اثم الاريسيين ويا اهل الكتاب
تعالوا الٰى كلمة سواء بيننا وبينكم
الا نعبد الا الله ولا نشرك به شيئاً
ولا يتخذ بعضنا بعضاً ارباباً من
دون الله فان تولوا فقولوا اشهدوا
بانّا مسلمون

Letter to Heraclius of Rome

Translation

In the Name of Allah Most Gracious Most Merciful.

From Muhammad servant and messenger of Allah to Heraclius Emperor of Rome.

Peace upon those who follow the Guidance.

I invite you to Islam; accept Islam, you will be safe, Allah will grant you two-fold reward; if you turn away, the sin of [the wrongdoings of] all the people will be upon you. O people of the Book: Come to an agreement between us and you that we worship none but Allah and that we shall associate no partners to Him, and that none of us shall take others for Lords beside Allah. And if they turn away, then say: Bear witness that we have surrendered to Him.

Muhammad messenger of Allah.

بسم الله الرّحمن الرّحيم
من محمّد رسول الله الٰى كسرى عظيم
فارس سلام على من اتبع الهدى
وامن بالله ورسوله وشهد ان لا
اله الا الله وانّى رسول الله الٰى
النّاس كافّة لينذر من كان حيّا
اسلم تسلم فان ابيت فعليك
اثم المجوس

Letter to Khosroe Pervez, Emperor of Persia

Translation

In the Name of Allah Most Gracious Most Merciful.

From Muhammad messenger of Allah to Kisra [Khosroe] Emperor of Persia.

Peace be upon those who follow the Guidance.

Believe in Allah and His Messenger and bear witness that there is no deity but Allah, the One Who has no partners and that Muhammad is His servant and His messenger. I invite you to the call of Allah for I am messenger of Allah to all the people so that I may warn those that are living. So accept Islam, you will be safe, but if you reject it, the sin of [the wrongdoing of] the Persians will be upon you.

Muhammad messenger of Allah.

- The Prophet sent letters (see p. 31) to the Roman emperor, the Persian emperor, the ruler of Egypt, the king of Abyssinia, the chiefs of Syria and various other leaders inviting them to accept Islam. Only the king of Abyssinia accepted him as the Prophet. Later, both the Roman emperor and the Persian emperor attacked Arabia in an attempt to destroy Islam and the Muslims. This happened during the last days of the Prophet.

THE CONQUEST OF MAKKAH (630 CE)

As the Quraysh had violated the Treaty of Hudaibiyah and the treaty was now void, the Prophet secretly planned an invasion of Makkah, and marched with an army of 10 000 Muslims. When this army reached the outskirts of Makkah, the Quraysh realised that they would not be able to resist this force. Abu Sufyān secretly met the Prophet and accepted Islam, and the Prophet declared that whoever took shelter at Abu Sufyān's house would be safe from attack. As a result there was hardly any bloodshed, and only 11 people were killed.

After the Muslim's victorious entry into Makkah, the first thing the Prophet did was to destroy all the idols and cleanse the house of God. As the Prophet was cleaning the Ka'ba of all the idols, he recited the Qur'ānic verse: 'We hurl the truth against falsehood and it prevails over it, and behold, falsehood vanishes away' (Qur'ān, 21:18).

After removing the idols, the Prophet asked Bilal, the slave who had become the *muadhdhin*, or *muezzin* (the person who summons Muslims to prayer), to give the *adhān* (call for prayer), and the Prophet then led the prayer, watched by the Quraysh. After prayer the Prophet called all the Quraysh people near the Ka'ba and asked them, 'What treatment do you expect from me?' They replied, 'You are a noble brother to the young and a gentle nephew to the aged.' And the Prophet said, 'I will treat you as Yusuf [Joseph] treated his brothers. You are free from all fear today. May Allah forgive you.'

When the Makkans heard this, they could not believe it. Then, when they realised that he meant what he said, they were overwhelmed with joy and gratitude. Within a short while they rushed to accept Islam.

The Prophet then addressed them and said:

> There is no diety but Allah, He is One and has no partner. He fulfilled His promise and Helped His servant and all by Himself crushed all the hosts. Today all the false prides and silly customs are trampled down under my feet. You are the children of Adam and Adam was created from dust. Allah says: O people! We have created you through a male and a female and have divided you into tribes and families so that you may know and distinguish one from the other. He is the gentlest amongst you that is most pious . . . Today Allah had forbidden the sale of liquor [and intoxicants], and usury.
>
> Ibn Ishaq, *The Life of Muhammad*

The Prophet asked the Muslims who had emigrated from Makkah to Medina not to reclaim any property they had left in Makkah now that they were back. He entrusted the key of the Ka'ba to 'Uthman bin Talha. He had once refused the Prophet entrance to the Ka'ba in the days before the migration to Medina and had ill-treated him. The Prophet said, 'If anyone takes the key of the Ka'ba from

'Uthman bin Talha or his descendants they will be cruel.' That is why the key is still in the same family to this day.

Eventually the other towns and tribes of the region followed the lead of Makkah and the whole of Arabia became Muslim.

?

1   Imagine that you are a citizen of Makkah. Write a letter to a friend in Jerusalem telling him/her how you expect to be treated when Muhammad (pbuh) captures the city and why.
2   When he captured Makkah, how did Muhammad (pbuh) show that a Muslim should be compassionate and merciful?
3   Why did the Prophet declare the Treaty of Hudaibiyah invalid?
4   Why was there so much warfare during Muhammad's (pbuh) time in Medina?

<table>
<tr><td>

Chapter
6

</td><td>

The Prophet's Departure

</td></tr>
</table>

THE FAREWELL PILGRIMAGE

After the conquest of Makkah and Taif, the Prophet returned to Medina. He stayed there for a year and then, in 10 AH (632 CE), he set out for his last and only pilgrimage (*hajj*). It is by performing this pilgrimage that the Prophet made known the rules of *hajj*, which are still followed by Muslims today (see Chapter 15).

Mount Arafat, where Muhammad (pbuh) gave his farewell sermon

THE LAST SERMON (*KHUTBAH*)

At Arafat the Prophet delivered his farewell sermon in front of 120 000 pilgrims. After praising and thanking Allah, he said:

> O people listen carefully to what I say because I do not know whether I would meet you again on such an occasion.
> O people regard the life and property of each Muslim as a sacred Trust just as you regard this month, this day and this city as sacred. Remember that you will have to appear before Allah and give an account of all.
> Return the things kept with you as a trust (*amānah*) to their rightful owners.
> All interest dues should be cancelled, you will give back only your capital. Allah has forbidden interest and I hereby cancel the interest dues payable to my uncle Abbas bin Abdul Muttalib.
> O people your wives have certain rights over you and you have certain rights over them. Treat them well and be kind to them as they are your partners and committed helpers.
> Beware of Satan, he is desperate in his attempts to divert you from the worship of Allah; so beware of him in all religious matters.
> O people listen with care. All believers are brothers. You are not allowed to take anything belonging to another Muslim unless he gives it to you willingly.
> O people none is superior to another unless it be in that person's obedience to Allah. No Arab is superior to non-Arab, unless it be in piety.
> O people reflect on what I am saying. I leave behind me two things – the Qur'ān, and my Sunnah. If you follow them you will not fail.

34

Listen to me carefully! Worship Allah, offer *salāh* [prayer], observe *sawm* [fasting] during the month of *Ramadān* and pay *zakāh* [money to the poor].

O people be mindful of those who work under you. Feed and clothe them as you feed and clothe yourselves.

O people! No prophet (*nabī*) or Messenger (*rasūl*) will come after me and no new faith will come.

All those who are listening to me should pass on my words to others and they to others again.

Have I conveyed to you the Message of Allah O people?

Ibn Ishaq, *The Life of Muhammad*

The Prophet looked towards the sky as he asked this question. The audience answered, 'Yes you have; Allah is the witness.'

When he had finished his sermon a revelation came to him:

Today I have perfected your religion
for you, and I have completed My blessing
upon you, and I have approved Islam for
your religion.

Qur'ān, 5:5

DEPARTURE FROM THIS EARTHLY LIFE

After returning to Medina, the Prophet fell ill. He became so ill that he could not lead the prayer or even, later, go to the mosque. At his command Abu Bakr started leading the prayer. According to what the Prophet said we learn that God had given him the choice of staying in the world or returning to Him. The Prophet preferred to return. His only surviving daughter, Fatima, was in great sorrow when she heard her father's decision. The Prophet comforted her by whispering that she would be the first of his relations to go to him.

When his death was announced in the mosque, 'Umar could not believe it. He thought the Prophet must be temporarily asleep and people were trying to create mischief, so he brought out his sword and threatened to kill anyone who said that the Prophet had died.

Abu Bakr went to the Prophet's house and then realised that he had indeed died. He returned to the mosque, looked at 'Umar, and then addressed the crowd with tears in his eyes:

Surely he who worships Muhammad should know that Muhammad is dead, but he who worships Allah should know that Allah is alive and never dies.

Then he recited the following verse of the Qur'ān:

Muhammad is naught but a Messenger; Messengers
have passed away before him. Why, if he should die
or is slain, will you turn about on your heels?
If any man should turn about on his heels, he will
not harm God in any way; and God will recompense
the thankful.

Qur'ān, 3:138

When he heard these words, 'Umar suddenly realised the truth of the Prophet's passing and he collapsed. At the same time, the Muslims felt reassured that Allah had not deserted them, even though the Prophet had left the world.

THE PROPHET'S FINAL ACHIEVEMENT

As we noted earlier, a prophet is a person selected by God through whom God tells humankind how to live and let others live in this world; what is harmful for human beings and what is good; what the relationship is between God, human beings and their environment; and how men and women should organise their lives so as to avoid mishaps and disaster and become God's true representatives on earth. Prophet Muhammad (pbuh) fulfilled this role.

He achieved his objectives through the messages that he received from God, by the example he gave in his own character and behaviour (see Chapter 7), and above all by the transformation of character that his example brought about in his followers.

The Prophet thus left for human beings a supreme example of the role of faith in human life. His life also embodied several important features of Islam:

● Islam demands complete self-surrender to God, and a readiness to be patient and able to accept suffering.

● Religion is seen as a complete way of life and has the authority to establish conditions in which such a way of life can be practised. This assurance was granted by God to the Prophet during his time in Makkah. Hence the establishment of the city state of Medina did not mean a change in his approach – it was a necessary consequence of the demand for the establishment of God's Kingdom on earth. The emigration from Makkah to Medina (Hijrah) was not a 'flight', but a planned withdrawal with the intention to set up a community where religion could be practised freely, where the message which reveals the truth of God could prevail over the hostility of the unbelievers who were guided by falsehood. 'Manifest victory' is seen in the Prophet's life as a clear indication of God's presence.

● *Jihād*, or fighting in the name of God, is an appropriate way of establishing the Truth. People should be ready to sacrifice life and property in this cause.

● Death is not seen as a tragedy. To die in the path of God is to gain the status of a martyr; but one must not fight simply in order to die, but to gain victory for God.

● Priority is seen to be given to the love of Truth. This is shown through love of God and the Prophet. *Jihād* is thus both a test and an example of a Muslim's love for Truth, in other words that person's *īmān* (faith).

?

1   Draw up a charter of human rights based on Muhammad's (pbuh) last sermon.
2   What anxieties about the Muslim community do you think concerned Muhammad (pbuh) as he faced death?
3   Why did Muhammad (pbuh) place a lot of emphasis on *jihād*?
4   **a**   When Muhammad (pbuh) died 'Umar was unwilling to accept the news. Why?
    b   Abu Bakr was equally insistent that Muslims should accept the fact that the Prophet was dead. Why?

<table>
<tr><td>

Chapter

7
</td><td>

The Prophet: The Ideal Human Being
</td></tr>
</table>

Muhammad (pbuh) was a historical figure. The Qur'ān, which contains all the messages sent by God to humankind through the Prophet, gives us a clear picture of him both as a natural human being, and as an ideal. His sayings and doings were recorded by many of his companions and later collected. These records cover social, political, economic, moral and spiritual aspects of life. They show that the Prophet was a perfect man, free from human weaknesses. He loved moderation, and advised all Muslims to avoid extremes and always to cultivate a balanced outlook. This balance does not mean a compromise. It means that a person should control his or her passions and desires, so that they do not take control of the person at any time.

The Qur'ān says that Muhammad (pbuh) is a man of 'mighty morality' (Qur'ān, 68:4), that is a person of very fine character. Jabir, a companion, reported the Prophet as saying, 'God has sent me to perfect good qualities and to complete good deeds.' The Qur'ān tells us how to be good – the Prophet exemplified that goodness. That was why when someone asked his wife, Ayesha, to say something about his character she replied that the Qur'ān was his character.

THE PROPHET'S QUALITIES

This chapter gives brief examples of some of the Prophet's qualities. When you have read it, find a biography of the Prophet (such as *Muhammad*, by Martin Lings) and look for other examples of his qualities.

Kindness

The Qur'ān tells us that God sent the Prophet as a mercy to all creation – *wa mā arsalnāka illā rahmatallil 'ālamīn* (I have not sent you except as mercy to entire creation). God's mercy was manifested through the Prophet. Muhammad (pbuh) was especially kind to the poor, to children, to slaves and to women, in other words to those who suffered most. He was also extremely kind to animals and even to plants.

To the poor
He used to pray, 'O God keep me alive as a poor man, make me die as a poor man and resurrect me in the company of the poor.' Abdullah ibn 'Amr al-'Ās said, 'Once I was sitting in the Prophet's mosque and the poor *muhājirūn* [emigrants from Makkah] were sitting in a circle in one part of the mosque. After some time, God's messenger [the Prophet] came and sat with them. On seeing this I got up and sat with them.' The Prophet said, 'Give good news to the poor *muhājirūn* that they will enter the garden of Paradise 40 years before the rich.'

To children

Anas said, 'I never prayed behind an *imām* who was more brief or more perfect in his prayer than God's messenger. If he heard a baby cry he would shorten the prayer for fear that the mother might be distressed.'

To slaves

The Prophet advised his companions not to say 'my slave' or 'my slave girl' but to say 'my son' or 'my daughter' instead. Someone asked him, 'How many times should I forgive a slave?' At first the Prophet was silent. When the person asked again, he replied, 'Forgive them 70 times a day.' He advised people to free their slave girls and then to marry them and not use them as concubines.

To women

'Umar reported, 'We did not have much regard for women in Makkah, but they were better treated in Medina. God's messenger established women's rights through his sayings and commandments, which strengthened their position and status.' (See Part III for more on family life and the position of women in Islam.)

To animals

The Prophet was extremely kind to animals. He stopped the cruel practices of cutting flesh from living animals or cooking them alive, of putting a ring around the neck of a camel, of shearing their hair or tails, of shooting arrows at animals, and of keeping animals in their working equipment for long periods of time. 'Don't make the backs of animals your chairs,' he said. Once a companion of the Prophet took an egg, which a bird had just laid, from the bird's nest. The bird began beating its wings in distress. The Prophet asked what was wrong, and when he learnt what had happened he made the companion put the egg back. He himself fed animals, tied camels and milked goats. He told his companions that a person who gave water to a thirsty dog and thus saved its life would be rewarded with a place in Heaven, and someone who starved their cat to death would go to Hell.

To orphans

Muhammad (pbuh) was himself an orphan. His feelings can be understood by this statement: 'If anyone pats an orphan's head, doing so only for God's sake, he will have blessings for every hair over which his hand has passed, and if anyone treats well an orphan girl or boy under his care, he and I shall be like these two in Paradise' (here he put two of his fingers together to show what he meant).

To enemies and unbelievers

An unbeliever came as the Prophet's guest one day and drank the milk of all his goats. That night the Prophet and his family went hungry. But he did not say a word to the guest or show any sign of anger. The Prophet tolerated everything he saw and all the taunts he heard.

Politeness

The Prophet always took the initiative in greeting other people. He even talked nicely to bad people so that they might be changed. He showed respect to elders. When his foster mother, Halima, came to see him, he spread his cloak out for her. No one who sat in his company ever felt that the Prophet was rude to them, or that he ignored or neglected them. He never turned his face away from the person he was talking to. He said, 'The people from among you who will sit close to me on the Day of Judgement are those who have good manners.'

Forgiveness, Love and Mercy

We have seen how forgiving the Prophet was to his worst enemies in Makkah. He was a living example of the Qur'ānic verse, 'Take the abundance, and bid to what is honourable, and turn away from the ignorant' (Qur'ān, 7:198). If anyone did evil to him, he did good to them in return. He used to say, 'God will not show mercy to him who does not show mercy to others.'

Generosity

Muhammad (pbuh) never said 'No' to anyone asking for help. One fifth of all the money gained after a victory was his share. He would distribute every single penny, and only after that would he go home. Once he borrowed half a *wasq* (an ancient unit of weight) of cereal for a beggar. When the lender wanted it back the Prophet gave him a full *wasq* – one half for the loan and one half as a gift. During the month of *Ramadān* he was even more generous.

The Prophet always paid the debts of the dead, and he told his companions to inform him of anyone who died leaving debts so that he could pay them.

All the above characteristics, and the true nature of the Prophet, are summed up in what he said to Ali, his son-in-law, about his own rules of conduct:

Abstinence is my avocation	Pleasure of Allah is my prize
Agony is my attendant	Intellect is the basis of my religion
Brotherly love is my method	Remembrance of Allah is my delight
Confidence is my asset	Revelation is my capital
Faith is my strength	Submission is my protection
Jihād is my career	Truth is my support
Knowledge is my weapon	Zeal is my horse
Patience is my dress	The light of my eye is *salāh* [prayer].

Hadīth

---

1   Give examples of the Prophet's forgiveness and love.

2   Try to find at least one event in the Prophet's life which demonstrates each of the rules of conduct listed in his words to Ali.

3   Muhammad (pbuh) is considered to be the perfect example of a Muslim. From this chapter and from Chapter 6, list the qualities that a Muslim should try to have. Discuss these with your neighbour. Then find out what other members of the class decided were the characteristics a Muslim might most seek to possess. Perhaps you could share your class's views with a Muslim and discover whether he or she agrees with you.

4   Islam is a very practical religion. How does Muhammad's (pbuh) life show this? Concentrate on generosity, children, forgiveness and poverty.

Chapter 8

The Spread of Islam

We have seen that Muslims had to fight a number of wars during the lifetime of the Prophet but none of these was for the purpose of spreading Islam. Even the conflict which led to the capture of Makkah was defensive. It was brought about because the people of Makkah had been harrassing Muslim traders and plotting against Medina. Wars continued after the Prophet's death, against the Byzantine and Persian Empires. These were also defensive, as were those against the Christian Crusaders.

Islam teaches that there is no compulsion in religion, so when Makkah and Jerusalem (in 635 CE) fell to Muslim armies their citizens were not forced to convert to Islam.

The wars which took place during the Prophet's lifetime and in the following century therefore:

● were started by non-Muslims; at first Muslims had to fight to save themselves, and, later on, to have power to resist the forces trying to destroy Islam,

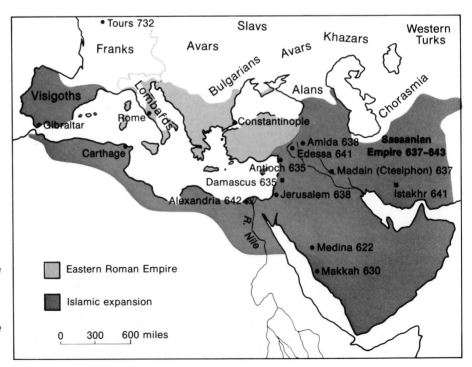

The expansion of Islam to 732 CE. In 710 Tariq ibn Ziyad led an army into Europe at a place now named after him, Gibraltar. In 732 a skirmish at Tours ended their push northwards into the Kingdom of the Franks. Muslim armies beseiged Constantinople in 716 but captured it only in 1400.

40

- were not used as a means to spread Islam, though it is true that conquests gave enormous opportunity to Muslims to spread Islam,

- are permitted in Islam to resist evil and even destroy it when it tries to destroy the good.

SPREADING ISLAM

Preaching by the Prophet

When the Prophet conquered Makkah, he did not force the Makkans to accept Islam. On the contrary, when they heard his preaching, they were overwhelmed by his generous forgiveness and gladly entered into the faith. Their own leader, Abu Sufyān, had already become a Muslim. The conquest of Makkah opened the eyes of the Makkans to the genuineness of the Prophet's call, the greatness of his mind and the benefits of peace, justice and truth.

Religious Toleration

After the conquest of Makkah the Muslims were powerful but the Prophet refused to allow force to be used to make people Muslims. There was a very large Christian community in the Yemen. He invited them to accept Islam but they refused, so Muhammad (pbuh) negotiated a settlement with the bishops of Yemen. They accepted Muslim rule but were allowed to retain their own religion and culture.

Missionary Work

When people find something new they usually want to share it. The companions of the Prophet found their new religion so satisfying that they began to preach it to the people around them. Two of them even crossed China and are buried in Beijing (Peking). Others made lesser journeys, to Istanbul and Thatta in Sind (now Pakistan).

Preaching by Saints and Scholars

Soon Islam began to produce learned scholars. These scholars also took the faith to other parts of the world. One of the most famous was Khwaja Muinuddin Chisti (1142–1236 CE) who converted many Hindus in India. They were persuaded by his arguments and his saintly character.

THE MUSLIM COMMUNITY: THE *UMMAH*

All those who follow Islam, the worldwide Muslim community, together form what is known as the *ummah*. They all follow the same faith, share the same basic values and are bound by their love of God and the Prophet, their obedience to the Qur'ān and the Sunnah (see also Chapter 9) and the practices of Muhammad (pbuh) and his personal teachings.

The *ummah* came into existence as a community with a common political authority when the Prophet established the city state of Medina. Those who lived outside Medina belonged spiritually to the same *ummah*, though politically they were living under different authorities. The same is true for all Muslims in the world today. Because of their common values, Muslims form one big community, and can mix with one another very easily even when they do not understand each others' languages. In public prayer Arabic is used worldwide and some people among each Muslim linguistic group know Arabic. They are the *'ulamā*, the learned people. They also bring the Muslims closer to each other. (Chapter 17 deals with the role and importance of the *ummah* to Muslims today.)

The Expansion of the *Ummah*

During the lifetime of the Prophet, nearly all the tribes of Arabia accepted Islam. Islam spread from one corner of the country to the other, until the whole of Arabia was under Muslim control.

After the Prophet's death in 632 CE, four of his closest companions ruled the country as Caliph (*Khalīfah*). The word 'caliph' means 'successor' or 'vice-regent'. These four Caliphs, also known as 'the righteous Caliphs' ruled during the following periods:

Abu Bakr	632–4 CE (11–13 AH)
'Umar	634–44 CE (13–23 AH)
'Uthman	644–56 CE (23–35 AH)
'Ali	656–61 CE (35–40 AH)

The office of *khalīfah* then went to two powerful Quraysh dynasties:

The Umayyad Dynasty	661–750 CE (40–132 AH)
The Abbasid Dynasty	750–1517 CE (132–656 AH)

Then the rule passed to the Ottoman Turks until 1924, when the system of Caliph rule was abolished by Turkey.

Outside Arabia, various independent Muslims ruled over different parts of the Muslim world, for example the Moghuls in India. But all of these rulers acknowledged the Caliph as the supreme head of the Muslim *ummah*; they paid dues annually to the Caliph, even though they were not under his authority.

1   What inspired many of the Prophet's companions to become missionaries?
2   What would attract those who met these missionaries to convert to Islam?
3   Imagine that you are a Muslim missionary. Write a *brief* sermon that you might preach to persuade someone to become a Muslim.

Part II   THE FOUNDATIONS OF ISLAM

Chapter 9

The Qur'ān and the Sunnah

Alif Lām Mīm

That is the book, wherein is no doubt,
a guidance to the godfearing
who believe in the Unseen.

Qur'ān, 2:1–2

It is naught but a Reminder
unto all beings.

Qur'ān, 81:26

Just before he died, the Prophet told the Muslims, 'I have bequeathed you two authorities, the Holy Book and my Sunnah.' The Holy Book is the Qur'ān which contains all the messages that God sent to Prophet Muhammad (pbuh). The Sunnah is the way of life shown by the Prophet through his sayings, doings and instructions, which are found in books known as Hadīth collections.

The Qur'ān and the Sunnah are the basic sources of the Islamic code of life followed by the Muslims. All Muslims revere them and regard them as the most precious things in their household.

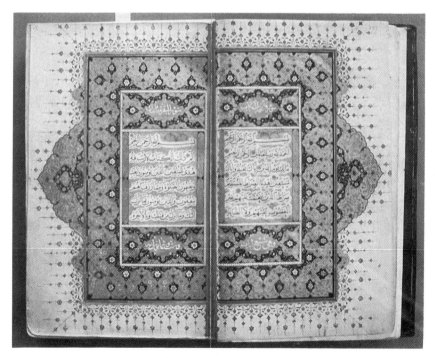

Pages from the Qur'ān

THE QUR'ĀN

The word *qur'ān* means 'reading' or 'recitation'. The word *āyāt* means *'signs'*. It is the name given to the verses of the Qur'ān.

The Qur'ān, the holy book of Islam, was revealed to the Prophet Muhammad (pbuh) by the angel Gabriel. The first verses were given to him in about 610 CE and the last shortly before he died. Sometimes Gabriel spoke to him as one man to another, and at other times it was like the ringing of a bell, which was painful for the Prophet. Some *āyāt* were long and he worried about being able to remember them correctly, but God told him not to be anxious, he would be given the ability to memorise them perfectly. The words of the Qur'ān are not Gabriel's or Muhammad's (pbuh). They are from God, given to help people to organise their lives for their good here and in the hereafter, and for the benefit of other human beings.

The 'revelations' that are now found in the Qur'ān were especially treated, from the very first revelation until the last, as forming part of one holy book (*kitāb*). This decision was not taken by the Prophet: he was instructed by God through Gabriel. Thus the Qur'ān is a book consisting of what God sent down to the Prophet through the angel Gabriel in the Arabic language that God himself had chosen for revealing His last most comprehensive guidance for human beings. The revelations provide a total world view.

Wahy (Revelation or Inspiration)

The word *wahy* comes from the Arabic verb *wahā*, which means 'to inspire'. It occurs in the Qur'ān in a number of shades of meaning. One meaning is the direct word of God revealed to the prophets, for example the Qur'ān.

Wahy also means inspiration arising from within individuals. Thus truth may come to people intuitively, giving them some guidance. That is what happened to the mother of Moses when she conceived the idea of sending baby Moses adrift in a basket (Qur'ān, 28:7). Even the instinctive actions of animals, birds or insects are regarded as having been inspired by God as the right thing to do. That is why the Qur'ān refers to bees being 'inspired' to build their hives in particular places (Qur'ān, 16:70).

Inspirations to human beings and other creatures are temporary, occasional and disjointed, but prophetic revelations, meant for total guidance, were continuous and comprehensive. Moses received the revelations in written form on stone tablets, although God also used to talk to him directly.

Prophet Muhammad (pbuh) experienced various inspired moments in his life, and also received various statements directly from God. But these statements were given the status of 'Holy statements' or 'Holy sayings' (*Hadīth Qudsī*); they do not form part of the Qur'ān.

The Qur'ān provides information about a number of prophets. Look up some of the following passages and make notes about each prophet:

Abraham 2:124–9; 21:51–73; 26:83–9. **Moses** 28:7–35. **Jesus** 19:16–36.

The Names of the Qur'ān

Various names given to the Qur'ān indicate different important aspects of it. It is referred to in some verses as *al-kitāb* (the scripture) (Qur'ān, 21:10). This indicates that it is one complete book and not a collection of disjointed verses. Other names given to the Qur'ān, and their meanings, are listed below:

al-furqān (the criterion)
al-dhikr (the reminder, remembrance)
al-tanzīl (that which has been sent down)
hudan lil-muttaqīn (guidance for the God-fearing)
al-shifā' (the curer)

al-nūr (the light)
al-bashīr (the announcer)
al-nazīr (the warner)
al-rahmah (the mercy)
al-majīd (the glorious)
al-mubārak (the blessing).

The Descent (*Nuzūl*) of the Qur'ān

The Qur'ān came down, through the angel Gabriel, during the last 23 years of the Prophet's life. It is said in chapter 97, however, that it came down *in totality* on the Night of Power (*Lailat al-Qadr*). Muslim theologians explain that on the Night of Power the Qur'ān came down to *Bait al-'Izza* (House of Glory) – a place in the sky around the earth – and that from here it came down over the period of 23 years into the spiritual heart (known in Arabic as the *qalb*) of the Prophet. Thus it came down from the timelessness of God into our physical world dominated by time.

The Makkan Chapters and the Medinite Chapters

Historically, the Qur'ān is divided into two sets of chapters. Those chapters (*sūrahs*) which were revealed to the Prophet before the Hijrah (the Prophet's migration to Medina) are known as the Makkan *sūrahs*. The chapters which were revealed after the Hijrah are known as the Medinite *sūrahs*.

The Makkan *sūrahs* are short, strong, and full of hope for reward and warning of punishment. They deal mainly with love, faith, loss of faith and misery, the essence of God and His Attributes, the essence of humanity and of the whole of creation. Very rarely they give details about ordering life in this world.

The Medinite *sūrahs* are generally longer. They cover all aspects of human life on this earth. After establishing a community based on religious, spiritual and moral principles, the Prophet needed direction from God as to how to organise the lives of the people in a comprehensive system. The Medinite chapters of the Qur'ān provide this guidance. The whole of the Islamic system of life, and hence its political, economic and social aspects, are dealt with in these chapters.

Muslims say that there cannot be two separate sides of life, one secular and the other religious. Divine guidance integrates the two parts into unity.

Arrangement, Preservation and Collection of the Qur'ān

The Qur'ān used by Muslims today is divided into 114 chapters (*sūrahs*). The verses (*āyāt*) of some of the long *sūrahs* were revealed to the Prophet at different times. As soon as he received the revelation, the Prophet would tell his companions where those verses should go. He did this following instructions from God which were sent either through the angel Gabriel or through direct inspiration. This is why it is claimed in the Qur'ān that the arrangement is God's. Each *sūrah* (except the ninth) begins with: 'In the name of God, the Merciful, the Compassionate.'

The Prophet always had with him a few companions who were given the task of writing down the verses as soon as he recited them. He also took measures to ensure that the revelations were preserved by asking some of his companions to learn the verses by heart so that they could teach them to others.

Memorisers of the Qur'ān came to be known as *huffāz*. The practice is still very popular today. Someone who has memorised the Qur'ān may put the title 'Hāfiz' before his name or 'Hāfizah' before her name. Each year during *Ramadān*, the month of fasting, the Prophet used to recite the entire Qur'ān (so far revealed). During the last year of his life, the Prophet recited the whole of the Qur'ān in its present final form. It is reported that in that year Gabriel made him recite it twice.

All the verses of the Qur'ān were kept in written form on various materials in the house of the Prophet. Many companions also prepared their own written versions. The revelations were also preserved, in order, in the memory of the *huffāz*. What was lacking was an authenticated, centrally preserved book. The *huffāz* had written thousands of copies to help them to teach new Muslims in far-flung areas, but there was not yet a definitive book.

The Qur'ān: the definitive version

After the Prophet's death, Abu Bakr (the first Caliph) followed the advice of 'Umar and assigned the task of preparing a definitive version of the Qur'ān in book form to a Medinite companion of the Prophet, Zaid bin Thabit. This man collected all available materials on which the revelations had been written and compared these written versions with the version in the memory of the *huffāz*. He then prepared the final master copy of the Qur'ān and sent it to Hafsah for safe-keeping. All the slips of paper, leather and bones, on which were written verses revealed at different times, were burnt and buried underground by 'Umar. The text of the Qur'ān thus prepared was exactly the same as the version recited by the Prophet before his death.

During the time of the third Caliph, 'Uthman, many copies were made from the master copy. They were sent to the governors of the different provinces of the then Muslim world. Some of these copies of the Qur'ān are still available. The copy at Topkapi museum in Istanbul is claimed to be the one 'Uthman was reading when he was assassinated.

The text of the Qur'ān which is used today is a copy of the version prepared by Zaid bin Thabit. No additions to or deductions from this version have been made. Thus the Qur'ān is as it was during the time of the Prophet.

N. J. Dawood, a recent scholar, in *The Koran*, has tried to rearrange the Qur'ān according to the way the verses came down. But Muslims do not accept this arrangement. Why do you think this is?

Reading or Recitation of the Qur'ān

Rules for readers of the Qur'ān

- **Purification**   According to the instruction of God, one must be clean and pure before beginning a reading of the Qur'ān. The reader must perform *wudū* (ablution), or have a bath (which is obligatory after sexual intercourse).

- **Beginning a reading**   The reader must say first in Arabic: 'I seek the protection of God from Satan, the Cursed One' (*a'ūdhubillāhi minashshayṭānir rajīm*). He or she must then say: 'I begin in the name of Allah, the Merciful, the Compassionate' (*bismillāhir rahmānir rahīm*), before starting to read or recite the Qur'ān.

- **Pronunciation**   Generally all Muslim children are taught to recite correctly. The method of pronouncing the Qur'ānic words and phrases correctly, and reciting the verses correctly, is called *tajwīd*. All children learn this when they learn how to read the Qur'ān.

The impact of recitation on believers

When the Qur'ān is recited in a Muslim assembly, everyone is silent. There is no talking or gossiping. Even those who do not understand the words are moved by the impact of the sound of the verses on their spirit. Those who do understand are transported into a deeper world of reality which is not easy to explain. Divine words have divine reverberations and divine influence.

Students learning the Qur'ān

A Qur'ān stand

Treatment of the Qur'ān

When the Qur'ān is not in use its owner will cover it in cloth and place it on a shelf above other books which may be in the room. The hands are washed or a full bath taken before handling it, so that the person does not commit a sin. For the same reason women do not touch the Qur'ān during menstruation. Often a copy is placed on a Qur'ān stand while it is being read so that it need not be handled unnecessarily. Worn out Qur'āns are never thrown away. They are buried completely under the earth or thrown deep into rivers with something heavy to pull them down.

1   Discuss the view that unless you treat a book as a physical object with respect you will not respect its contents.

2   How might a Muslim respond to someone who said that it isn't necessary to treat a copy of the Qur'ān as something special?

The Language and Form of the Qur'ān

The Qur'ānic Arabic

All messages to the earlier prophets were sent in the language of the people to whom the prophets were sent. As Prophet Muhammad (pbuh) was an Arab, God chose the Arabic language to reveal the Qur'ān. It was a unique form of Arabic, however, with a structure and rhythm not found in the Arabic of the day. Poets were challenged to produce a single verse equal in merit to the words of the Qur'ān, but they failed to do so.

As we have seen, the Prophet was illiterate. This unique Arabic language, its rhythm and its deep message could not therefore have been produced by him. This is how the Qur'ān justifies its claim to have been revealed by God to the Prophet, rather than to have been created by the Prophet.

The unique form

The Qur'ān is not a history book and so the stories in it are not in chronological order. Nor is it a book of philosophy, and so the arrangement does not show the logical growth of an argument leading to a conclusion. Nor is it simply a book explaining rules and regulations. The Qur'ān cannot even be called a poetry book whose purpose is to rouse feelings and, through that, to make people conscious of some truth. It is more than this. It is an all-comprehensive work. It uses poetic, scientific, logical, discursive and intuitive methods to awaken within the believers' minds a consciousness of reality. Its own unique rhythm (not found anywhere else in the Arabic language and literature) varies along with the theme, and does not follow any metrical pattern.

The Basic Themes of the Qur'ān: the Essence of Islam

The content of the Qur'ān may be divided into the following six 'Truths':

● The Essence of God,
● The Essence of His Names and Attributes,
● God's Works,
● The Essence of human beings: their nature and purpose,
● The straight path and the reward of following it in this world and in the hereafter,
● The crooked path and the consequence of following it in this world and in the hereafter.

Through these six items the Qur'ān presents to human beings a comprehensive way of life. This vision of life covers human existence from before a person's creation to his or her final judgement. The way of life shows the integral relationship between faith in One unique God and the moral and spiritual progress of the human being.

The Hidden Meaning of the Qur'ān

It is said in the Qur'ān that its verses have an outer and an inner meaning. In order to understand the inner meaning, scholars have decided that we must see:

● whether the Prophet has said anything about these verses,
● whether any companion of the Prophet has said anything on them,
● whether any highly learned Muslim scholar (*'alim*) has given any interpretation which is widely accepted.

Allegorical and symbolic verses and disjointed letters

The Qur'ān contains some allegorical verses, and Arabic letters at the beginning of several chapters, whose meanings seem to be rather secret. Only God knows the significance of these. Ibn Abbas, a cousin and companion of the Prophet, said that some spiritually learned people may be granted this knowledge by God.

Science of the Qur'ān

A Qur'ānic science started growing during the lifetime of the Prophet. Today it has become huge. Not only is there now the science of reading (*tajwīd*), there are also the sciences of recitation (*qirā'ah*) and of interpretation (*tafsīr*). Anyone who wants to understand the Qur'ān must know the Arabic language thoroughly, must have read all the Hadīth literature, and be familiar with all previous interpretations.

?

1 Why has so much attention been given to the Qur'ān by Muslims?
2 Why do Muslims insist that only someone who can read the Qur'ān in Arabic can really understand it?
3 Why was Muhammad (pbuh) so overwhelmed when he received a revelation?
4 How do you think a Muslim feels when he or she becomes *hāfiz* (i.e. able to recite the whole Qur'ān by heart)? Imagine you are a Muslim and write a letter explaining these feelings to a non-Muslim friend.

THE SUNNAH

All that Muhammad (pbuh) did or said or instructed as part of Islam is regarded as the Sunnah of the Prophet. It is obligatory for all Muslims to follow it.

Instructions that are found in the Qur'ān are direct instructions from God. Any additional item that the Prophet instructed is Sunnah. For example, the command to pray, and the times for prayer, are laid down in the Qur'ān (*sūrahs* 4:103; 11:114 and 17:78–80); so, too, is the requirement to wash before praying (*sūrah* 5:9). But the prayer positions are not laid down in the Qur'ān. They were taught to Muhammad by the angel Gabriel, and the Prophet passed them on to his companions. The prayer positions, then, come from the Prophet's Sunnah, not from the Qur'ān.

Sources of the Sunnah

The Sunnah can be learnt from two sources: the Hadīth collections and the *Sīrah* (a biography of the Prophet).

Hadīth collections

'Hadīth' means 'a saying'. The Hadīth collections are the original source of the Sunnah, though they contain not only the Prophet's sayings but also reports about his doings and the doings of his close companions.

The Sīrah

In order to learn the Sunnah, scholars started to gather together all the information available about the Prophet's life. The earliest known *Sīrah* (biography) is by Ibn Hisham. A shortened version of this, by Ibn Ishaq, is available in English translation.

SHARĪʿAH

The Qur'ān and the Sunnah together provide Muslims with guidance in living their lives. In the early days of Islam, they were compiled in the form of rules and regulations by eminent scholars. The resulting 'code of conduct' is known as Sharīʿah. In English, the word may be translated as 'path'. It has formed the basis of the legal code of some Muslim countries, for example Saudi Arabia. (Chapter 16 discusses Sharīʿah in more detail.)

1   What is a biography? Why did Muslims think that it was important to write a biography of the Prophet soon after his death?

2   How might the sayings (Hadīth) and practices (Sunnah) of the Prophet help people to become better Muslims?

Beliefs

There are seven essential beliefs that a Muslim must hold. These are in:

● God,

● the angels who serve God,

● the books or messages sent by God through prophets to human beings for their guidance,

● the prophets who preached these messages, from the first prophet Adam to the last prophet Muhammad (peace be upon them),

● the Day of Judgement or Last Day, when the entire creation will be destroyed by God and recreated in a new form, and when all spirits will be sent back to resurrected bodies,

● life after death, including the Day of Judgement when God will decide the destiny of human beings, that is who will go to Paradise and who will go to Hell,

● God as the ultimate authority decreeing what will happen to anyone and anything in this creation, including human beings.

This is known as a Muslim's *īmān*, which means faith (not to be confused with the Arabic word *imām*, which means the leader of prayers).

BELIEF IN GOD The Unity (*tawhīd*) of God is the central doctrine of Islam. This is perceived and explained in three different ways:

The Unity of Essence

This Unity transcends all Qualities. It is the Unity of Essence that possesses all Qualities. Each Quality limits God to one aspect in our perception. But He is above and beyond all Qualities. Human beings are asked to worship that Essence. Nothing is like Him:

> He is God, One,
> God, the Everlasting Refuge,
> who has not begotten, and has not been begotten,
> and equal to Him is not any one.

> Qur'ān, 112

The Essence of God is totally Transcendent. It has nine characteristics:

● God's necessary existence: He alone exists, that is why He can bring creation into being,

- God's Being from all eternity: He has no beginning, the creation has,

- God's Being for all eternity: He has no end, the creation has,

- God's Essentiality: All essences come from Him,

- God's Uniqueness: He is Incomparable,

- God's Unsubstantiality: substance is created,

- God's Unembodiedness: body is a material substance. His Essence has no material body,

- God's Formlessness: He has no form,

- God's Omnipresence: His presence is felt everywhere.

The Unity of Absolute Qualities

Muslims perceive God through His Qualities. God possesses Qualities which He uses in order to create and then to sustain creation, to destroy it, alter it, change it or modify it. God is the Creator, the Sustainer, the Destroyer. He is the Merciful, the Just, the Truth, the All-Knowing. Therefore absolute mercy, justice, truth and knowledge belong to Him only. All these qualities are eternal. Amid the many qualities, the Muslim is aware of the One who possesses them.

These qualities provide human beings with the highest example of the norms by which they should live. For example, justice should be absolute and universal so there should be no favouritism or discrimination of rich or poor, black or white. God also exercises His Qualities in a balanced way so that Justice is tempered with Mercy, the destructive power with His sustaining power. If it were otherwise, the universe would be destroyed.

The Qualities of Allah are expressed through His names (*asmā'*). Though He is Allah, the One, there are also 99 'beautiful names' which are applied to Him, which express His Qualities. When a Muslim prays, a name may be chosen from these 99 and the believer will receive the particular grace (*barakah*) associated with that name.

The Unity of God's Works

Muslims believe, as we have seen, in the Unity of God. God is consistent. It follows, therefore, that His creation, the universe, reflects this Unity. Sometimes human beings may find it difficult to see and understand, but as they grow in faith they find their awareness improves.

For example, they see that the beauty of the rose comes from God. Its beauty *may* seem to die as the flower fades but it is reflected in another rose as well as other beings. These are all signs of Allah (*āyātullāh*) which submit to the Laws of God which scientists call the Laws of Nature.

> and to Him has surrendered whoso is in the heavens
> and the earth, willingly or unwillingly, and to Him
> they shall be returned?
>
> Qur'ān, 3:77

God is the real cause of everything. He also sustains the universe. He hasn't left it to run itself. To the Muslim, natural calamities such as earthquakes, floods and hurricanes are part of God's order. This suffering has a purpose. It warns people of their evil ways so that they may turn to the path of obedience.

? If Allah's Will is manifest in His creation, if everything in this creation reminds us of a Quality of Allah, why should we not worship each object?

Relationship between God and Human Beings: Faith

Faith in God is 'natural' for human beings. It is natural to love God more than anything or anyone else. Our spirit demands it because, according to the Qur'ān, our spirit has come from God's spirit. That is why God says in the Qur'ān that He is nearer to a person than that person's own neck vein.

Anyone who does not believe in God is therefore doing something 'unnatural'. They are harming themselves. People who believe in something other than the Transcendental Unity of God are also misleading themselves. Faith in God means faith in this Transcendental Unity, faith in the Absoluteness of God's Attributes and Qualities, and faith in His Total control of the whole of creation. Human beings have within themselves that spirit which is beyond space and time and which naturally responds to God.

BELIEF IN ANGELS

A Muslim believes in angels (*malāikah*). They are not material but ethereal beings. They are Allah's creatures, made out of light. They are Allah's agents or servants: Allah runs the universe with them. In other words, the angels fulfil the commands of Allah. They are invisible to human beings but they can assume any form they choose. The angel Gabriel was seen by Prophet Muhammad in human form. The angels are sexless and immortal. They do not enjoy the freedom that a human being enjoys. It is not possible for a human being to describe their real form, though the Qur'ān mentions that they are God's 'messengers having wings two, three and four' (Qur'ān, 35:1).

Some angels perform special functions, and thus have special status.

- Gabriel brings Allah's message to the prophets. He also has a life-giving quality granted by Allah. It is he who came to the Virgin Mary, according to the Qur'ān, and passed on the spirit to the Virgin by spiritual means. That is how the Virgin Mary conceived Jesus.

- The angel Michael is the life-sustaining angel distributing life and food to every creature in the universe.

- Azra'il is the angel of death.

- Isfrafil is in charge of the final destruction of the universe.

- Malik is in charge of Hell, with 19 angels under him.

- Ridwan is in charge of Paradise.

- Two angels are constantly recording our deeds.

- Bad deeds are wiped out if we ask God's forgiveness. That is why two angels are known as *Kirāman Kātibīn* (The Two Generous Writers).

- Two Angels will ask a dead person about his or her faith; they are known as Munkar and Nakir.

Angels pray to God to forgive the offences of believers (Qur'ān, 21:103; 13:24, 33,43).

BELIEF IN HOLY BOOKS

A Muslim believes that God sent messages through some of His prophets so that people may know what is good for them or what is bad for them and act accordingly so that they may go to Paradise and not suffer in Hell. These messages are known as the Holy Books.

Of these books only four are mentioned in the Qur'ān. They are:

- *Tawrāt* **(the Torah)** revealed to Moses (Mūsā),

- *Zabūr* **(the Psalms)** revealed to David (Dāwūd),

- *Injīl* **(the Gospels)** revealed to Jesus,

- *Qur'ān* revealed to Prophet Muhammad (pbuh).

A Muslim cannot accept the present versions of the first three of these books because, it is claimed in the Qur'ān, the followers of those religions have suppressed, added and altered many things in their books. They are no longer pure. This is why the Qur'ān had to be revealed. One of the purposes of the Qur'ān is to restore to mankind the Original Revealed Truth.

A Muslim's belief in the holy books implies that people have received the same truth or message from all the prophets from Adam to Muhammad (pbuh). There is thus a continuity in God's message and the Qur'ān is the final most comprehensive version of that message. God will preserve it in its pure form until the Last Day. This is why Muslims believe that human beings do not need another messenger or another book.

BELIEF IN PROPHETS

As we have seen, Muslims believe that God reveals Himself through prophets, or messengers. Some prophets received God's messages, others followed them.

Each new message from God included within it all earlier messages. To reject that new messenger or prophet was to reject truth. Jews who denied Jesus when he came, rejected truth. Similarly, those who rejected the Prophet Muhammad (pbuh) also rejected truth, though they may be Jews or Christians.

A Muslim's belief in prophethood also implies the following:

- Human history is divided into two periods, pre-Muhammad and post-Muhammad. The time of prophethood came to an end with Muhammad (pbuh). He, therefore, is the final and supreme example (*al-uswat al-hasanah*) for the rest of humanity until Doomsday. The message revealed through him is the final most comprehensive message for all people.

- Islam is the only religion that will survive, and the whole of humanity will one day become Muslim.

- All prophets were people who never deliberately committed sins. They were protected from sin by God, but they sometimes made mistakes. The Qur'ān describes Adam's disobedience as the result of error and forgetfulness caused by satanic temptation, and not deliberate. Moses' killing of a person was also not deliberate; he intended to chastise, not to kill. Abraham tried to hide the truth, he did not tell a lie.

- There are various stories in the Hebrew Bible about Jewish prophets committing grave sins. Muslims point to the Qur'ān and say that the Qur'ān considers these stories to have been made up by men, and not to be revelations from God. According to Islam, all prophets have the same quality of *'ismah*, meaning that they did not commit any sin either before or after they were informed of their prophethood.

- Every prophet had the following seven characteristics:
  - trustworthiness
  - truthfulness and devotion
  - the mission of communicating God's message
  - justness
  - purity from sin
  - super-intelligence
  - security against dismissal from prophethood

- Prophethood cannot be attained by human effort. When God created human beings, He decided who He would send as His prophets, and which of those would receive His message.

- The same reverence must be shown to all the prophets.

- All the prophets should be accepted by believers, whether their names are mentioned in the Qur'ān or not. The orthodox Muslim view is that believers should accept all prophets whose names Allah has mentioned, but they should not dispute over those whose names God has not mentioned. As God is silent about them, Muslims should be silent about them also.

The Prophets

Of the total number of prophets (either 140 000 or 240 000, according to the Hadīth), 313 or 315 of them actually received messages from God. These prophets were the *rasūl* (messengers). Seven of them are known as *ulul 'azm* (the great prophets). Peace be upon them all. They are:

- Adam,
- Nūh (Noah),
- Ibrāhīm (Abraham),
- Mūsā (Moses),
- Dāwūd (David),
- 'Īsa (Jesus),
- Muhammad.

The Qur'ān mentions 26 other prophets by name, for example: Ayyūb (Job), Ismā'īl (Ishmael) and Ishāq (Isaac). The names of the many other prophets, sent to each other part of the world, are not given in the Qur'ān.

Practices

Though the basic beliefs were the same, some of the practices of the various prophets were different. This is admitted in the Qur'ān. That is why there was a difference about the Sabbath day, which was assigned to the Jews but not to the Muslims. Some kind of fasting was prescribed in all earlier religions, but fasting for one whole month was prescribed only for the Muslims. Only Muslims are expected to pray five times a day. God has allowed these differences in practices but insisted on the same beliefs. During the time of Prophet Muhammad (pbuh), these beliefs became confused, and a complete purification of people's minds and the restoration of original beliefs became a necessity. That is why a Muslim believes that keeping the message given to the prophet Muhammad (pbuh) amounts to keeping those of all previous prophets from Adam to Muhammad (pbuh).

BELIEF IN THE DAY OF JUDGEMENT

Muslims believe that the entire creation, including this world, will one day be destroyed by God and rebuilt in a new form. That day is known as the Last Day (*qiyāmah*) or the Day of Judgement (*yawmuddīn*). Various early *sūrahs* describe this total destruction (Qur'ān, 81:1–14; 82:1–19 and 69:13–37).

No one knows the exact timing of this Last Day, not even Muhammad (pbuh). When Gabriel asked him, he replied that Gabriel knew as much as he knew. When he was asked what would signal the coming of the Last Day, he said: 'Slaves shall be masters and black people will be building very tall houses.' The other signs are: the coming of *Imām Mahdī* (the guided one), the coming of *Dajjāl* (the anti-Christ) and the return of Christ to kill *Dajjāl*, to purify the entire world and to preach Islam.

A Muslim's belief in the Day of Judgement also implies the following:

● After the total destruction there will be a resurrection of all creatures. This resurrection is of the body as well as the spirit or essence. In other words, not a single particle of any individual ever gets lost. They come together when Allah calls them.

● Muslims believe that people are responsible for their own actions in this world. This also means, therefore, a belief in the freedom of human will.

● A record of each Muslim's deeds is kept by the angels. The record (Book of Deeds) will be handed over on the Last Day.

BELIEF IN LIFE AFTER DEATH

Belief in the Day of Judgement leads to belief in life after death (*ākhirah*) and how people will be treated after the Last Day (Qur'ān, 21:49). This involves belief in *Jannah* (Paradise) and *Jahannam* (Hell). The Qur'ān is full of references to these and gives concepts and images of reward and punishment.

Muslims believe that there is progress in an individual's relationship with God during their stay in Heaven or Hell. Life after resurrection is a journey to draw closer and closer to God. Even Hell will be purged of a large number of people after they have been purified through suffering.

Human life on earth is, therefore, not an end in itself. But actions in this life will be the cause of reward or punishment in the afterlife. Moreover, if someone prays for the dead, the dead person will get the benefit immediately.

Muslims believe the hereafter is a real place. Life in this world is temporary, even though most people act as if material possessions have lasting worth. In between death and the Last Day, or the Day of Judgement, there is a stage through which all spirits have to pass. If souls remain attached to this world, then they continue to suffer. Pure souls enjoy bliss. The Hadīth also speak of a divine balance to weigh human activity and a bridge over which each soul must pass – a bridge thinner than hair and sharper than the sword.

BELIEF IN PREDESTI-NATION

God is the final master who decides everything. Fate is decided for each individual even before his or her birth. Where a person will be born, when that person will die, even the minutest details of a person's life are decreed by God. This is predestination (*qadr*).

God, however, is not bound by what He has decreed. He has given human beings freedom of choice, and He can change whatever He wants to change. That is why human action is considered so very important for each individual and for each community.

When a companion asked the Prophet why, if everything is predestined, people should bother doing good deeds, the Prophet replied: 'Do you know what has been decided for you?' In other words, we should act not with the idea that our activities are meaningless, but with the idea that we shall get reward or punishment as a result of what we are doing. We should also act in the knowledge that Allah has given us freedom of choice, a power not granted to the sun or the moon or natural objects or creatures which follow the natural laws ordained for them by God.

?

1   Why is the Day of Judgement an important Muslim belief?

2   If everything has been decided before we are born, what is the point in doing anything – good or bad? How would a Muslim answer this question? (When you have thought about it, you might be able to invite a Muslim to school to discuss your answers with you.)

3   One of the biggest problems facing religious people is the question of how God can be all-powerful and yet human beings have free will. Discuss the problem, writing the issues in your notebook. Then, imagine you are a Muslim, write a short letter to a friend explaining the Muslim view. Perhaps you could put together an actual class letter and send it to a Muslim for comment. (You would need to send a general letter too explaining your interest in the matter – and remember to send a stamped and addressed envelope for a reply.)

Chapter 11

The Five Pillars

The following story sums up the essence of Islam.

Islam in a Nutshell

The Caliph 'Umar said:

One day when we were with God's messenger, a man with very white clothing and very black hair came up to us. No mark of travel was on him, and none of us recognised him. Sitting down beside the Prophet, leaning his knees against his, and placing his hands on his thighs, he said: 'Tell me, Muhammad, about Islam.'

The Prophet replied, 'Islam means that you should testify that there is no god but God and Muhammad is God's messenger, that you should observe the prayer, pay the *zakāh*, fast during *Ramadān*, and make the pilgrimage to the Ka'ba if you have the means to go.'

The man in white said, 'You have spoken the truth.'

We were surprised at his questioning the Prophet and then declaring that he had spoken the truth.

He said to the Prophet, 'Now tell me about *īmān*.'

The Prophet replied, 'It means that you should believe in God, His angels, His books, His prophets and the Last Day, and that you should believe in the decreeing of both good and evil.'

Remarking that he had spoken the truth, the man in white then said: 'Now tell me about *ihsān*.'

The Prophet replied, 'It means that you should worship God as though you saw Him, for He sees you though you do not see Him.'

The man in white then went away and after I had waited for a long time the Prophet said to me, 'Do you know who the questioner was, 'Umar?' I replied, 'God and His messenger know best.' He said, 'He was Gabriel who came to teach you your religion.'

This quotation is from the Hadīth (a collection of Prophet Muhammad's sayings and doings).

---

1   Why is it that Gabriel comes to question Muhammad (pbuh)?
2   What is the purpose of this Hadīth?

'Umar was one of the Prophet's senior companions. After the Prophet's death he became the second Caliph (or ruler) of the Muslim world.

In Chapter 10, we discussed *īmān* (faith or belief). Without faith, no one can be called a Muslim. We shall now look at the foundations of Islam, or, as Prophet Muhammad (pbuh) called them, the Pillars of Islam. These 'pillars' – bearing witness, prayer, payment of tax to the poor, fasting and pilgrimage – provide the spiritual basis of Islam.

The Five Pillars of Islam

- **Shahādah**: to bear witness that there is no god but God and that Muhammad (pbuh) is His messenger,

- **Salāh** (prayer): to pray five times a day,

- **Zakāh** (almsgiving): a fixed amount to be paid in charity by the end of each year,

- **Sawm**: fasting for the whole lunar month of *Ramadān*,

- **Hajj**: pilgrimage to Makkah and Arafat if one can afford to go and do it.

THE SIGNIFICANCE OF THE FIVE PILLARS

Each of the five pillars is a form of worship in itself. Yet, together, they form a comprehensive structure. To remove one is to harm the total structure. It is very rare to find a Muslim who says his or her prayers regularly, but who does not fast or who does not (if that person has wealth) pay *zakāh*.

Hajj is the only one of the five pillars which may be difficult for some Muslims to carry out, since it is the only one that demands a certain amount of money. However, even the poorest Muslim, who says his or her prayers, fasts, and pays *zakāh*, intends to go to Makkah and Medina at least once in his or her lifetime. It is a thought that is constantly alive in the heart of all Muslims.

The five pillars of Islam are the basis of an entire way of life for a Muslim. They lay the foundations of faith and goodness in the human soul. They strengthen the love of God and the Prophet. At the same time, they strengthen the believer's power of resistance to forces of evil and destruction. Like the Prophet, a Muslim wants to be compassionate to the poor, the needy and orphans, and to be strong, hard and decisive against unbeliefs, temptations and vices. The experience of *hajj* (pilgrimage) teaches a Muslim what true egalitarianism is.

Thus the five pillars create the true Islamic personality and become the foundation of the entire moral fabric of the individual and the community.

?

1   The first pillar is a statement of belief, the other four have to do with practices. What does this tell us about the relationship of faith and action in Islam?

2   One meaning of Islam is 'surrender'. How do the four pillars of action enable Muslims to show this?

3   Discuss the view that the five pillars are an excellent example of the link which Islam forges between duty to God and duty to one's fellow human beings.

4   Some people say that they should be able to worship God when they like and as they like. Islam stresses the need for discipline. Think of reasons Muslims might put forward to support their view, and write them down now. When you have studied the sections on prayer (Chapter 12), and the poor due (*zakāh*) and fasting (Chapter 14), reconsider your answer.

5   **a**   How do the four pillars (other than *shahādah*) combine in forming the character of a Muslim?

    b   What characteristics or qualities of God are developed in a Muslim who faithfully keeps these pillars?

Shahādah *and* Salāh

This and the next three chapters will look at each of the five pillars of Islam in more detail.

THE FIRST PILLAR: *SHAHĀDAH* (BEARING WITNESS)

All Muslims bear witness in their heart (*qalb*). In public, Muslims use these words: 'I bear witness that there is no god but God and Prophet Muhammad is his Messenger.'

'Bearing witness', however, is not simply a matter of saying words, although it is true that making this statement of faith is the only thing that a person wishing to become a Muslim initially needs to do. Bearing witness means being convinced in your deepest self that God exists and putting your trust in Him. It also means being so convinced that Muhammad (pbuh) was Allah's Prophet that you become transformed by being like him. As Muhammad (pbuh) loved truth, justice and mercy, and gave his life fully to God, so too will those who love and respect him try to follow his example.

When we read the history of the early Muslims we see what happened to people when faith entered their hearts. Look back, for example, to Chapter 3 'The conversion of 'Umar'. When 'Umar followed his sister's instructions to wash, become clean and read the verses from the Qur'ān, he changed. Faith and love entered his heart. It was then that he went to the Prophet, accepted his leadership and started obeying him.

The relationship between following (*ittibā'*) the Prophet and loving God is so intimate that Allah told the Prophet to tell the believers: 'If you love God, follow me, and God will love you' (Qur'ān, 3:29).

THE SECOND PILLAR: *SALĀH* (PRAYER)

The English word 'prayer' does not indicate all that is meant by *salāh*. *Salāh* is a very distinctive system. It cannot be performed if you are unclean and impure, and so Muslims must know how to make themselves clean and pure. The Arabic word for this is *tahārah*, which means purification through ritual cleansing. This *tahārah* also means something very specific.

Muslims are taught that there is a difference between everyday washing (i.e. keeping clean and washing away dirt) and becoming clean and purified for *salāh* (prayer). Ritual cleansing is done in such a way that it is a mental as well as a physical cleansing – being mentally prepared for prayer is very important in Islam.

Ritual cleansing and purification (*tahārah*) has two forms: *wudū* (ablution) and *ghusl* (bath).

Wudū

The form of wudū

The method of cleansing oneself externally (the form of *wudū*) is very simple. These are the instructions that a Muslim performing *wudū* will follow. They derive from the teaching and practices of the Prophet.

> Wash your hands up to the wrists thrice; rinse your mouth three times with water thrown into your mouth with your right hand; sniff water into the nostrils and expel it three times; wash the entire face, including the forehead three times; wipe the head once with the inner surface of the fingers of both hands together; put two forefingers into the two ears and wipe the back of the ears with the thumbs; and with the backs of the fingers of both hands wipe the back of the neck once; wash the right foot and then the left foot up to the ankles three times.

The meaning of wudū

The intention of this cleansing is to purify the body and soul. While washing the hands and the mouth, the person doing *wudū* should pray to God that they may be purified from the stain of the sins that they might have committed with their hands or mouth, either knowingly or unknowingly. While washing the nostrils, the person must pray that they are made pure enough to savour the sweet scent of Heaven. While washing the face, the person must pray to God to remove the darkness of sin covering their face and bathe it with God's own light. While washing the right arm, the person must pray to God to give the Book of Deeds in their right arm as will be done to the righteous on the Day of Judgement (the Book of Deeds is the record kept of each individual by the angels). While washing the left arm, the person must pray to God not to place the Book in it (because that is the treatment that the unrighteous will get). While wiping the head, the person must beseech God to cover the head with His Mercy. While cleaning the ears, the person should beseech God to purify the heart so that the ears do not desire to hear bad things. Whilst wiping the back of the neck, the person should beseech God not to hurl the 'throne of His Curse' on the neck as will be done to Satan. While washing the right foot, the

person should pray to be guided in the right and straight path. While washing the left foot, the person should pray not to be led astray into the path of misguided people. In this way, *wudū* becomes an act of worship in itself.

Men performing wudū *– the practice remains essentially the same, regardless of time or place*

How long does wudū *last?*

Wudū is made invalid by deep sleep, unconsciousness and natural discharges from the body. If any of these things happen, a Muslim must repeat his or her *wudū*. So long as none of the above things happen, Muslims may say their prayers without having to perform *wudū* again.

Ghusl

In certain circumstances, a full bath (*ghusl*) is necessary. Washing the whole body is obligatory after:

- sexual intercourse,
- menstruation, and post-natal confinement when a woman has given birth to a child,
- wet dreams.

Privacy is very important in *ghusl*. If *ghusl* is to be a means of purifying yourself, you cannot be naked in front of anyone. That is why communal bathing or showering, as is the custom in many Western schools, is forbidden in Islam.

Concessions or Exceptions Relating to *Wudū* and *Ghusl*

In the following cases, certain concessions, exemptions and alternative arrangements are permitted:

- If water is not available while a person is travelling, then the person is exempted from *wudū* and *ghusl* and is allowed instead to do the following: strike the palms of the hands on dry earth, stone or sand, then brush the hands together, then rub the face, the hands and the arms. This is known as *tayammum*.

- People with skin diseases which might become worse if water touches the skin are not required to wash the affected parts of their body.

- If washing the feet becomes difficult in certain situations, people are allowed to wipe over their socks.

- If doing *wudū* may aggravate an illness, a person is permitted to do *tayammum* (see above) instead.

Final Preparation for Prayer

Before praying, Muslims must have an intention to pray. This is called *niyyah*. Together with *wudū*, it should prevent a Muslim from praying in a thoughtless manner.

Timing of Prayer

Muslims must say their prayers five times a day. The timing of daily prayers is as follows:

Morning prayer (*salāh al-fajr*)	Between dawn and sunrise.
Midday prayer (*salāh al-zuhr*)	Between midday and halfway between midday and sunset.
Afternoon prayer (*salāh al-'asr*)	Between midday prayer and sunset.
Evening prayer (*salāh al-maghrib*)	After sunset till darkness covers the twilight.
Night prayer (*salāh al-'ishā'*)	Between evening prayer and dawn.

?   Suggest reasons why the five prayer times occur at the times outlined.

Form of Prayer

Units

Units are the series of words and actions used by Muslims when they pray. There is a fixed number of obligatory units (*rak'ah*) in each prayer. They are as follows:

Morning prayer	2 units
Midday prayer	4 units
Afternoon prayer	4 units
Evening prayer	3 units
Night prayer	4 units

Extra units were added by the Prophet, and these are known as *Sunnah rak'ah*. Scholars consider some of these to be more binding than others. There is, however, some variation in the rules because there was also variation in the Prophet's practice.

Postures

There are four basic postures which are always followed in a Muslim's prayer:

Positions of prayer: bowing (above) . . .

- **Standing (*qiyām*)**   The right hand is clasped lightly above the left wrist with the hands just above the waist. (Some groups of Muslims allow their hands to hang straight down by their thighs.)

- **Bowing (*rukū'*)**   The hands are placed on the knees.

- **Prostration (*sujūd*)**   The forehead and nose touch the floor, the fingers face the *qiblah* and the elbows are raised.

- **Sitting (*julūs*)**   The left leg and foot are folded under the body and the right foot erect resting on fingers turned towards the *qiblah*; in another posture the feet are folded under the body; in the third posture the bottom touches the floor, the left foot is folded under the body and the right foot is stretched sideways to the right.

. . . prostrating (left), sitting (right)

Other Rules of Prayer

As well as the need for ritual cleansing (*wudū* and *ghusl*) and the need to declare an intention (*niyyah*) to pray, there are other rules which a Muslim must also follow:

- First the call for prayer (*adhān*) must be given (see Chapter 4).

- The clothes the person is wearing must be clean and pure (even dirt from the road will destroy the purity of the clothes).

- The place must be clean. If the place is dry, a clean and pure piece of cloth or carpet can be spread out, so that the person can pray on that.

- The worshipper must face towards the Holy Ka'ba.

- Worshippers must first decide mentally which prayer they are going to offer, and realise that they are before God, facing in the direction (*qiblah*) of the Ka'ba.

- If there is a group of people, they must select the most learned and elderly person, someone who follows Sharī'ah properly, as the *imām* to lead the prayer.

- If there are only two people, they should stand side by side, the *imām* on the left of the other person.

- If there are more than two, then the *imām* stands in front and the others make rows behind.

- The person who gave the call to prayer now recites a second call to prayer (*iqāmah*) and everyone comes into line so that prayer may begin.

Praying on a prayer carpet

The Meaning of Prayer

When Muslims pray, standing with bent heads and crossed arms, like slaves in front of their master, they see God within their hearts. If they are not yet as spiritually developed as this, they are at least mentally aware of the Ka'ba which they are facing, and they imagine that Allah is in front of them. In this upright position, they recite the opening chapter of the Qur'ān (the *Fātihah*):

In the Name of God, the Merciful, the Compassionate

Praise belongs to God, the Lord of all Being [the worlds],
the All-merciful, the All-compassionate,
the Master of the Day of Doom.

You only we serve; to You alone we pray for succour.
Guide us in the straight path,
the path of those whom You have blessed,
not of those against whom You are wrathful,
nor of those who are astray.

Qur'ān, 1

The first half of this *sūrah* (chapter) is exclusively about Allah, and as the worshippers recite the words they think about God's qualities. The second half is about each individual who is praying. Muhammad (pbuh), however, said that a spiritual dialogue takes place between Allah and the servant who prays as these words are said. God responds to the servant who worships Him by assuring him or her that the petition will be granted.

The reciting of this *sūrah* in formal prayers is essential because for each of the verses uttered by the worshipper God gives a reply.

After this, the worshippers then recite some more verses of the Qur'ān. It is expected that they would pay attention to the meaning of the verses as they recite them. The worshippers then bow and recite at least three times, 'Glory to my God, the great!' As they straighten up, the *imām* says aloud, 'Allah hears those who love Him.' The congregation replies, either silently or aloud, 'Our Lord, praise be to Thee.'

Prostrating themselves, the worshippers say again, 'Glory to my God, the greatest of the great.' They should forget themselves completely. Then they sit in the posture of humble slaves, hands held out to God, offering prayers for themselves, their families and descendants.

Finally, while in the same position, they turn their faces to the right and then to the left, saying each time, 'Peace and God's blessings be upon you.' In this way they ask that Allah may bless not only those who are with them in the mosque but all humanity and the entire creation.

The actual saying of prayers lasts only a few minutes on each of the five occasions. It is not length that matters, but the discipline of remembering God so that eventually He is permanently in the Muslim's mind, and the discipline of concentrating on the acts of preparation and of saying the prayers. Of course a Muslim may turn to God at any time and in any place to pray about matters of personal concern.

Women may pray in the mosque, but not in the same room as the men so that there are no distractions to interfere with concentration. They are not required to attend the mosque, however, though the obligation to pray five times a day is the same for women as it is for men. It begins at the time of puberty.

Devotion in Prayer

Praying in a mosque in Britain

Prayer of Ali: self-annihilation

Ali, the son-in-law of the Prophet, used to forget his whole self when he started praying. Once, in a *jihād*, the head of an enemy's spear broke off in his heel. Some companions wanted to pull it out, but the pain was so intense that Ali would not let them. The Prophet secretly asked one of his companions to wait until Ali prostrated himself in prayer, and then to pull the spear head out quickly. The companion did as the Prophet said, and Ali did not feel it at all. He continued to pray. Afterwards, even though he saw the blood and he felt acute pain, he also felt relieved.

Prayer of Hatem Asam: concentration

Hatem Asam was a great Muslim saint, a companion of the Prophet's companions. When someone asked him how he prayed, he said: 'I feel Allah's presence in front of me. I think death is standing behind me to take me away at any moment. I think of the righteous on my right, and satanic people on my left. I regard myself as completely alone with no one to help me except Allah. That is what gives me concentration in prayer.'

1   Discuss why Muslims consider careful preparation for prayer to be so important.
2   Imagine that you are a Muslim.
   a   What reasons would you give for following a precise form of words and actions at *salāh*?
   b   Describe how you would feel if your employer would not allow you time for saying your prayers. Put your reasons into a polite letter.
3   Prayers should not be said precisely at the time the sun is rising or setting. Can you think of reasons for this? You may need to refer to an earlier chapter.

The Mosque and the Friday Congregational Prayer

Chapter 13

You read in Chapter 4 that the first thing the Prophet did when he reached Medina was to build a mosque. That mosque is now known as *al-Masjid al-Nabawī*, or the Prophet's mosque. Even today, wherever Muslims go, the first thing they do is to set up a mosque just as the Prophet did in Medina.

Mosques in Britain

When I first came to Britain in 1949 there were two mosques: one in Woking and one in East London. Now there are more than a thousand. Some are big and beautiful – like the one in Regent's Park, the rebuilt East London mosque, the Birmingham mosque and the Dewsbury mosque – and some are small. For the sake of the small Muslim community in north Cambridge, I had to turn a room in a house into a temporary prayer room so that it could be used as a mosque. This is how mosques first began to be set up in Britain.

THE MOSQUE

As you enter a mosque, you will notice that there are no images of any living figure anywhere. Muslims believe that if such images were allowed in the mosque, people would be encouraged to worship them instead of God's greatness. Instead you will find the words Allah and Muhammad, and also some verses of the Qur'ān, written in beautiful Arabic calligraphy on the front wall, perhaps also on the side walls, or on sheets of paper which are hung on the walls. This emptiness means that Allah is present everywhere.

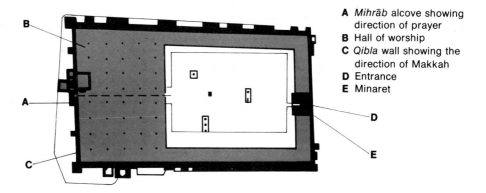

A *Mihrāb* alcove showing direction of prayer
B Hall of worship
C *Qibla* wall showing the direction of Makkah
D Entrance
E Minaret

Plan of a mosque

Qiblah

The next thing to attract your attention is the direction towards which all Muslims pray. *Qiblah* means direction. The true *qiblah* is God, who is in front of every worshipper. The worshippers must try to feel His presence. In order to have a common *qiblah* for all, the Ka'ba was made the *qiblah* by God after the Prophet went to Medina. That is why all mosques are constructed in such a way that one side of the rectangle faces in that direction. This is known as the *qiblah* wall.

Mihrāb

In mosque architecture, there is a niche in the middle of the *qiblah* wall which is physically outside the wall. The *imām* stands there to lead the prayer. The design of Muslim prayer rugs often represents the *mihrāb* or niche in the mosque that marks the direction of prayer.

Minbar

Beside the *mihrāb* there is a small staircase with three or four steps. This is known as the *minbar*. The Prophet made this so that he could stand on a slightly raised platform to enable the worshippers to see him when he gave his two sermons on a Friday. This is the place where the *imām* stands to deliver his sermon.

Khutbah *(speech or sermon)*

Any sermon can be described as a *khutbah*. But generally the term is used for the two Friday sermons given one after the other, which are known as the Friday *khutbah* or just as *khutbah*.

Imām

The *imām* is the person who leads the prayer. Whenever there are at least two Muslims gathering to pray, the one who has a better knowledge of the Qur'ān or who is the older and who is a better practising Muslim should act as the *imām*.

If you go to a mosque nowadays you may well meet an *imām*. We have said that he is simply one who leads the prayers. That is true, but now he is often a learned man appointed by the local community (this is always the case in Britain), or the government, to give spiritual guidance, organise its affairs and probably teach children Arabic, how to read the Qur'ān, and the Muslim faith.

Mosque of Ibn Tulun (876–9 CE), Cairo

The Madrasa mosque and mausoleum of Sultan Hassan (1356–61 CE), Cairo

Mosque of Hagia Sophia, Istanbul

THE FRIDAY CONGREGATIONAL PRAYER

O believers, when proclamation is made for prayer on
the Day of Congregation, hasten to God's remembrance
and leave trafficking aside; that is better for you,
did you but know.
Then, when the prayer is finished, scatter in the land
and seek God's bounty, and remember God frequently;
haply you will prosper.

Qur'ān, 62:9-10

This passage from the Qur'ān mentions specifically the 'Day of Congregation' (Friday). Because of this, even those Muslims who are a bit negligent about the other daily prayers try to go to the mosque on Fridays.

According to Islamic belief, God prescribed for Muslims not a whole day for services and prayer like the Jewish Sabbath or the Christian Sunday, but a congregational prayer at midday on Friday. All Muslims must then get together in the mosque as soon as the call for prayer is given. They must give up whatever worldly activities they are doing. When they have gathered in the mosque, a second call for prayer is given. Then the *imām* gets up and stands on the *minbar*, which is always placed on the right side of the *mihrāb*, to lead the prayer.

The *imām* then gives two sermons. After giving the first sermon he sits on the staircase (*minbar*) for a minute or two and then gets up and gives the second sermon. All sermons must ultimately draw the attention of all those assembled in the mosque to the glory and greatness of God and the Prophet and the necessity of leading a life of righteousness and piety.

After the two sermons, the *imām* leads a prayer consisting of two *rak'ah* only. After this prayer, people pray individually. They can then leave the mosque and go back to their daily routine work.

It is obligatory for all adult male Muslims to join in this congregational prayer and listen to the sermons. Women may or may not attend. It is considered spiritually highly beneficial. The Prophet said, 'This is the day when Adam (pbuh) was created. This was the day when he was sent to the earth. This was the day when he died. There is a certain moment in this day when God gives a person whatever that person wants, provided the person does not want an unlawful thing.'

?

1   Look at the role of the *imām* as described in this chapter. Why has it evolved from being a prayer leader to being a man who performs many other functions?

2   Why do you think that Muslims who came to Britain quickly established mosques? Why did they need a place of their own for prayer?

3   What is the value of having a special prayer day?

4   What reasons are there for Muslims having Friday as their 'Day of Congregation'?

5   **a**   In groups organise a discussion between a Muslim, his or her employer, and a trade union official, in which three Muslims ask for permission to pray in the mosque at noon on Fridays but the employer is not sympathetic. Argue each position as well as you can. The task of the trade union official is to try to see both sides but to help the Muslim member by suggesting solutions.

    b   Your request has been turned down. Write a letter to a relative in Egypt describing your feelings at not being able to observe the requirement to pray in the mosque.

    c   Your request has been granted on appeal. Write a second letter.

<table>
<tr><td>

Chapter

14
</td><td>

Zakāh *and* Sawm
</td></tr>
</table>

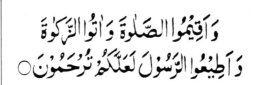

Perform the prayer, and pay the alms,
and obey the Messenger – haply so
you will find mercy.

Qur'ān, 24:55

The Meaning of *Zakāh*

The Arabic word *zakāh* means purity. It also means growth, blessing and development. In actual fact, *zakāh* means the payment of a certain percentage of one's remaining wealth at the end of the year to the poor and the needy – in other words, a 'poor tax'. Instructions about this tax are given in the Qur'ān. Muslims believe that through payment of *zakāh* they will attain blessing and spiritual growth, but how can this payment of money purify a person? It does so in the following ways:

- A person's wealth or property is considered in Islam to be a trust given by God to that person for his or her own use and also for the society in which he or she lives. By giving money to the poor and the needy, a person with some wealth is fulfilling an obligation.

- If the person does not pay *zakāh*, he or she will be regarded as a hoarder. Hoarding is prohibited in Islam. Paying *zakāh* allows a person's wealth to circulate in society. Thus, by paying the money, a person purifies himself or herself and also purifies his or her wealth by paying from it what should go to those who deserve it.

- By paying *zakāh*, a person purifies his or her own heart from greed and miserliness, and purifies the heart of the recipient from jealousy and hatred.

- By accepting *zakāh*, the poor and the needy are doing something to help the rich.

Zakāh is not a state tax, though it used to be collected by the state authority during the days of the Prophet and the caliphs, and, according to Islamic law, the state still has the authority to collect *zakāh* and distribute the money among certain categories of people listed in the Qur'ān (see below). In most Muslim states today, *zakāh* has become something personal. It is a test of sincerity, for only the givers know how well off they are and whether they are paying what they should. Thus it makes demands on a Muslim's honesty as well as on his or her purse.

Who Pays *Zakāh*

Every Muslim who owns something beyond basic needs at the end of the year should pay *zakāh*. The amount to pay is based on the 'excess' wealth of that person, the produce of their land, their cattle, and any precious metals, for example gold and silver, that they own.

How Much to Pay

The rates are fixed as follows:

On money and savings	$2\frac{1}{2}\%$
On the produce of land:	
if irrigated naturally	10%
if irrigated by hand or machine	5%
On windfall assets	20%
On precious metals (except jewellery worn regularly, e.g. certain rings)	$7\frac{1}{2}\%$

When to Pay

The common rule is that *zakāh* should be paid at the end of every lunar year. Exceptions to this rule are (a) *zakāh* on a treasure or a windfall asset (e.g. a gift or bequest) should be paid immediately and (b) *zakāh* on land produce should be paid straight after harvesting. Generally Muslims pay *zakāh* in the month of *Ramadān*, because they get special *barakah* (grace from God) if they pay during that month.

To Whom *Zakāh* Should be Paid

The Qur'ān (9:60) lists eight categories of people who deserve *zakāh*:

● the poor,
● the needy who do not ask,
● those who have been employed by the authorities of a country to collect *zakāh*,
● people who embrace Islam and are in need,
● slaves and prisoners of war so that they may be freed,
● people who have fallen in debt because of some disaster,
● travellers in difficulty,
● those who do not have time to earn their living because they are engaged in missionary work.

Priority must be given to near relatives who fall into any of these categories.

1   Deciding how much to give is not always easy. In Britain, for example, a Muslim family might look at its savings – say £10 000. They should give away $2\frac{1}{2}$ per cent of this, i.e. £250. But what if they also receive a £1000 bonus (after tax £750)? Is this income or a windfall? How might the family decide? What would you give your money to?

- the mosque building fund
- an orphanage in Tunisia
- Sudanese famine relief
- a local hospice for the terminally ill.

Imagine that you are this family. How would you decide? (Use role play to arrive at your answer.)

2   How does *zakāh* help in the redistribution of wealth?

3   Muslims must not lend, borrow or invest money at interest. What is the economic value of this?

THE FOURTH PILLAR: *SAWM* (FASTING)

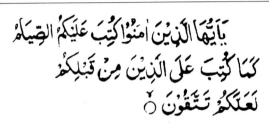

O believers, prescribed for you is the Fast, even as it was prescribed for those that were before you – haply you will be godfearing.

Qur'ān, 2:179

The Meaning of Fasting

Fasting is complete abstinence. It is both physical and mental. Physically, a Muslim abstains completely from food, drink, smoking and sexual intercourse from dawn to sunset during the whole of the month of *Ramadān*, the ninth lunar month in the Islamic calendar. Mentally, a Muslim must abstain from indulging in backbiting, violence, greed, lust, anger and other such passions, and thus control his or her emotions and desires. The purpose of fasting is therefore both physical and mental self-discipline.

During *Ramadān*, a Muslim may act as usual between sunset and dawn, but he or she is prohibited from over-indulging in food, drink and smoking in an effort to make up for abstinence during the daytime. Muslims are expected to learn self-control through fasting.

Who Should Fast

All Muslim boys and girls who have reached adolescence must fast during *Ramadān*. Fasting is obligatory for every Muslim adult, with the following exceptions:

- those who are ill or physically weak and unable to fast because of illness or weakness,
- women during their monthly cycle. On medical grounds women may also be exempted temporarily during pregnancy and when they are breast-feeding.

People in these two categories are exempted from fasting only temporarily. They should make up later. Permanent exemption is granted to those who will not be able to make up later because of specific disabilities. Such people must feed a poor person for every day that they miss a fast.

Muslims in the Polar Regions

Since the daylight hours vary so much in the extreme north or south, Muslim jurists have decided that there should be special rules regarding the duration of fasting for Muslims living in these areas. It has been decided that they may fast either the same number of hours that a nearby Muslim community outside the arctic zone or antarctic zone fasts, or the same number of hours that the people of Makkah would be fasting during that year.

Special Significance of *Ramadān*

The month of *Ramadān* is regarded as a specially blessed month. Allah's mercy is poured out during this month and those who fast enjoy this bliss. Those who give charity during *Ramadān* receive special grace from God. Other special features of this month of fasting are listed below:

- **Suhūr** This Arabic word is used throughout the Muslim world. It means pre-dawn meal. The Prophet told the Muslims that such a meal is a blessed thing, and so all Muslims enjoy a pre-dawn meal during *Ramadān*. In the villages of Bangladesh, for example, men and women get up just after midnight. Women cook the meal and men read the Qur'ān or say voluntary prayers.

- **Tarāwīh prayers** The *tarāwīh* prayer is said only during the month of *Ramadān*. It is said after the night prayer (the *'ishā'* prayer) in congregations in mosques all over the world. The Prophet used to finish reciting the whole of the Qur'ān during this prayer. Today, in most of the mosques of the world, *huffāz* are appointed to lead this prayer and to finish reciting the whole of the Qur'ān during this prayer within the month of fasting.

- **Lailat al-Qadr** This means the Night of Power. It is one of the odd numbered nights from among the last ten days of *Ramadān*. According to the Qur'ān, if someone stays awake throughout this night and spends the night in prayer and meditation, he or she gets the benefit of keeping awake and praying for one thousand nights. Generally, all mosques remain full during this night.

- **I'tikāf (seclusion for religious work)** A person will get God's special blessing if he or she goes into total seclusion for a few days. It is generally male Muslims who do this. Quite often they stay in the mosques for at least three days during the last ten days of *Ramadān*.

The month of *Ramadān* thus provides Muslims with the opportunity to earn a large amount of blessings through their activities. In a number of countries, Muslims do not sleep at all until dawn. They go to bed only after the morning prayer, and get up a little later than usual but without allowing their work to suffer.

Nadia's Fasting

Nadia is a young Muslim girl. She lives in London with her parents and goes to secondary school. Here she describes her fasting.

'As I grew up, I saw my father and mother getting up in the middle of the night to do something. I wanted to be with them. They tried to dissuade me and make me stay in bed. I wouldn't. They told me that they were going to fast from the next day. My father told me that this was the month of *Ramadān*. I was only five. I thought fasting was a nice new thing. I said I would like to fast also. My mother smiled and said, "All right, then you must have some *suhūr*."
"What is *suhūr*?" I asked.
"We eat something before dawn. That is what our Prophet told us to do. All Muslims do that," said my mother.
"All right, give me some *suhūr*," I said.

'*Suhūr*, I thought, was some special meal. But it was just what we eat at breakfast. I drank only a cup of milk. I was feeling sleepy, so my mother put me to bed. I learnt later that they read the Qur'ān till dawn, said their morning prayer and then went to bed.

'In the morning I decided to fast. My mother didn't say anything. She waited till I was very hungry and I started crying. She pacified me by saying that for a girl of my age two hours of fasting was accepted by God. So I was happy.

'Now that I am 14, I have started fasting for the whole month of *Ramadān*. From the age of seven I started fasting for a day or two. Gradually I was allowed to increase the number of days. Last year I nearly completed the month. This year I have. In future I must, as I am a grown-up girl.

'For the first two or three days I feel hungry, but afterwards I get used to fasting. It is even enjoyable, especially in the evening when we break our fast. We prepare nice salty and sweet things, put them on the table and wait for the sun to set.

'My mother comes from Bangladesh but I have never been there during *Ramadān*. She tells me that she used to do the same with her mother and sisters and brothers. They used to wait to hear the *adhān* from the mosques. I imagine it must be romantic to hear so many *adhāns* and all the people saying prayers and then breaking their fast with special things made for them. Though we do not hear the *adhān* here it is also nice to wait like that with food in front of you and then pray and break the fast. Then we invite some of our relatives and friends to come and break their fast with us, say the *maghrib* prayer and then eat our dinner together. It is great fun. My studies do not suffer at all; the only thing I don't like doing in the daytime when I am fasting is playing games or running about.'

1   How do the rules of fasting show God's compassion?
2   How does fasting help Muslims to develop attitudes of compassion?

Chapter 15

Hajj

THE FIFTH PILLAR: *HAJJ* (PILGRIMAGE)

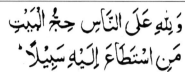

وَبِلهِ عَلَى النَّاسِ حِجُّ الْبَيْتِ
مَنِ اسْتَطَاعَ إِلَيْهِ سَبِيلًا

It is the duty of all men towards God to come to the House a pilgrim, if he is able to make his way there.

Qur'ān, 3:91

The *hajj* is the pilgrimage to the Ka'ba and other holy places at Makkah. It takes place in the twelfth month of the Muslim year, *Dhul Hijja*. All Muslims want to perform *hajj* at least once in their lifetime. But *hajj* is meant only for those who can afford to make the journey and who can withstand the physical strain. Lots of poor people save money throughout their life so that they will have enough to perform *hajj* at least once, but by the time they can afford to go, they are already old. Some people who perform *hajj* in their old age think that if they die and are buried in Makkah or Medina they will go to meet God as a servant of God who has been purified through *hajj*.

Why Muslims Perform *Hajj*

The main purpose of *hajj* is to get Allah's forgiveness, to become once again as pure and innocent as a newborn child. It is said that, after their fall, Adam and Eve went under God's instruction to the plain of Arafat near Makkah where they prayed together and were forgiven by God. The place where they were supposed to have prayed between afternoon and sunset is marked on a hillock in Arafat. This hillock is therefore known as the hillock of mercy (*jabal ar-rahmah*). That is why all pilgrims go to Arafat and weep and pray throughout the day, especially during that time between afternoon and evening.

The plain of Arafat

... hidden from my eyes in the midst of this lifeless wilderness of valleys and hills, lies the plain of Arafat, on which all the pilgrims who come to Mecca assemble on one day of the year as a reminder of that Last Assembly, when man will have to answer to his Creator for all he has done in life. How often have I stood there myself, bareheaded, in the white pilgrim garb, among a multitude of white-garbed, bareheaded pilgrims from three continents, our faces turned toward the Jabal ar-Rahma – the Mount of Mercy – which rises out of the vast plain: standing and waiting through the noon, through the afternoon, reflecting upon that inescapable Day, 'when you will be exposed to view, and no secret of yours will remain concealed' ...

As I stand on the hillcrest and gaze down toward the invisible Plain of Arafat, the moonlit blueness of the landscape before me, so dead a moment ago, suddenly comes to life with the currents of all the human lives that have passed through it and is filled with the eerie voices of the millions of men and women who have walked or ridden between Mecca and Arafat in over thirteen hundred pilgrimages for over thirteen hundred years . . . I hear the sounds of their passed-away days, the wings of faith which have drawn them together to this land of rocks and sand and seeming deadness beat again with the warmth of life over the arc of centuries, and the mighty wingbeat draws me into its orbit and draws my own passed-away days into the present, and once again I am riding over the plain . . .

Muhammad Asad, *The Road to Mecca*

THE RITES OF *HAJJ*

A *hājjī* is a man who has completed *hajj*. A woman who has completed *hajj* is known as a *hājjah*. According to Muslim teaching, God has laid down certain rites for all pilgrims. Of these rites, four are obligatory. The first is the putting on of *ihrām* (special clothes), the second is doing the *tawāf* (circling) of the Ka'ba, the third is to go to Arafat, and the fourth is the last *tawāf* of the Ka'ba after returning from Arafat. These important rites are each described in detail on the following pages.

THE PROCESS OF *HAJJ*

Intention (*Niyyah*)

The first thing the pilgrims do is to decide whether they are going to Makkah for *hajj* or with some other intention (*niyyah*). Once their hearts are clearly set for *hajj*,

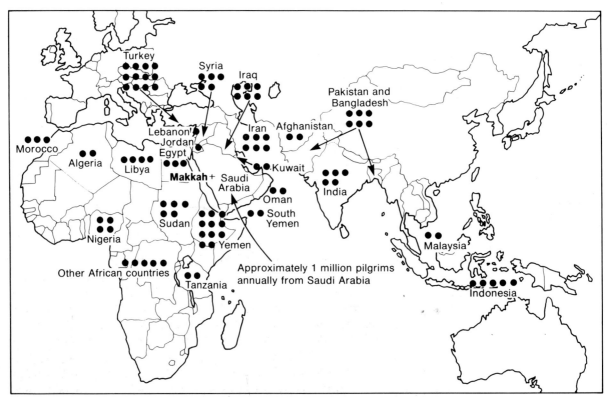

The countries from which most Muslims go on the hajj*. Each dot represents 1 per cent of the total of 3 500 000 pilgrims (e.g. about 70 000 come from Tanzania). About a million pilgrims are from Saudi Arabia.*

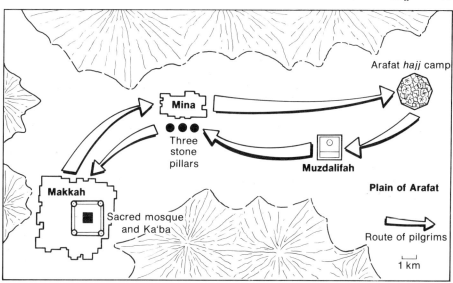

The route of the hajj

their job is half done. Even if a sincere person dies on their way to Makkah, God will say that they achieved the *hajj* and will get the benefit of it each year until Doomsday.

The hājjīs *who could not go to Makkah*

There was once a man and his wife who had saved enough money perform *hajj*. The day before they were to buy their tickets and set out for *hajj* they visited a poor friend and found him and his family almost starving. They gave the money they had saved for *hajj* to this family, and so they could not go. Some other friends of the couple, who had gone before them, then saw the man and his wife in Makkah. When they came back and learnt what had happened, they realised that God had accepted the intention of the couple and given them the full benefit of the *hajj* and forgiven all their sins.

Ihrām

Before reaching Makkah, pilgrims must put on special clothes. Women and girls wear plain loose dresses that cover their whole body except for their faces, hands and feet. Men and boys wear two unsewn pieces of white cloth, one round their body from waist to ankle and the other over their shoulders. There are certain areas round Makkah, known as *mīqāt*, where pilgrims should put on *ihrām*, say two *rak'ahs* of prayer and ask God's help to perform the *hajj*. In fact, most of those who travel by plane put on their *ihrām* before boarding. They say the two *rak'ahs* when they cross into the *mīqāt*. Once they do so, sexual intercourse and killing animals or insects become *harām* or forbidden. They then start thinking of submitting themselves wholeheartedly to God's Will. This is the meaning of wearing *ihrām*. It is the first obligatory rite of *hajj*.

Men wearing ihrām

Talbiyah

As soon as the pilgrims reach Makkah, they start reciting the *talbiyah*:

Labbayka, Allāhumma labbayka	I am here, O God, I am here.
Labbayka, lā sharīka laka labbayka	I am here, You are without companion, I am here!
Innal-hamda wan-ni'mata laka wal-mulk	Praise and blessings are yours, and dominions!
Lā sharīka laka	You are without companion!

The word *labbayka* means 'I do obey You, I am at Your service.' It implies 'I have obeyed You, O Lord, and I am at Your service.' It further implies 'I will obey You, and be at Your disposal, as a thing which You shall dispose of with Your hands in whatever manner You shall please.'

Imagine thousands and thousands of people forgetting the world, their homes and their relatives and all their worldly problems, and singing this song loudly as they rush towards Makkah, enter it and proceed towards the Ka'ba, the house of God, which they have dreamt about visiting at least once in their lifetime. That is what *hajj* is like!

Tawāf

As the pilgrims enter Makkah they have just one intention. That is to go round the Ka'ba seven times (*tawāf*). They start either by kissing the Black Stone (*al-hajar al-aswad*) which is fixed at the eastern corner of the house or by raising their hands towards it and reciting a prayer. They then go round the Ka'ba in an anti-clockwise direction. Each circuit is done in the same way. *Tawāf* is the second obligatory rite of *hajj*.

The Ka'ba

The Ka'ba is the first house of God, and was built by Adam. 'Ka'ba' means a cube. It is said that Adam built a triangular room without a roof or cover so that a throne sent down by God could be placed inside it. The throne had a white stone on it, emanating light. One day after Adam's death the stone vanished into Adam's grave. Then, during the time of Noah, the Ka'ba itself was washed away. It was rebuilt in the same place by Abraham with the help of his son Isma'il. But they built it as a rectangular room, one side of which was of a half-crescent shape.

The present Ka'ba has been rebuilt several times, but always on the same foundations. Some of the original stones have been used along with new ones. Abraham, like Adam, had built it without a roof, but when the people of Makkah first rebuilt it they added a wooden roof to shelter it from the rain. The pieces of wood, however, were not big enough to cover the whole room and so they had to build a new wall on the crescent side. They kept the crescent space marked by a low wall.

The Ka'ba is covered by a specially sewn black cloth on which is embroidered the words 'There is no god but God' and 'Muhammad is God's Prophet' as well as some Qur'ānic verses. Some verses are embroidered with golden thread. This covering is known as *kiswa*.

Muslims feel veneration for the Ka'ba, but they do not worship it. They feel a great sense of *barakah* (God's grace or blessings) when they are near it. It is a place where many prophets had come and millions of worshippers had prayed even before Muhammad (pbuh) started preaching Islam.

Pilgrims circling the Ka'ba during hajj *or* 'umrah

Kissing the Black Stone (al-hajar al-aswad)

'Umrah

After performing *tawāf*, the pilgrims stand in front of the only door of the Ka'ba and say a short prayer. Then they drink water from the Zamzam well near the Ka'ba before going to do *sa'ī*. *Sa'ī* means walking seven times between two small hillocks, Safa and Marwah. *Tawāf* is a practice from the days of Adam. *Sa'ī* was installed by Abraham in commemoration of what Isma'il's mother, Hagar, did (see p. 80). The two observances complete what is known as *'umrah*.

Hagar, Isma'il and Zamzam

Hagar was the slave girl whom Abraham married with the permission of his wife Sarah. He had a son by her, Isma'il – his first son. But after a few months Abraham was instructed by God to take Hagar and Isma'il from Canaan to Makkah, where he left them with a bag of dates and a leather bag of water. When Hagar asked him why he was doing this, Abraham said that God had told him to. Although there was no human habitation and no water, Hagar believed that God would help her.

When she had finished all the water and still felt thirsty, she left the baby and went to the nearby hillocks known as Safa and Marwah in order to see whether there was any water nearby. Seven times she ran and walked from one hill to the other. Then she heard someone calling and she saw an angel pointing to Isma'il. She ran and saw that a spring had gushed out where the baby was kicking the sand. She said '*zam zam*' ('stop stop') and built a hole with the sand and stones around it. That is how the well came to be called Zamzam.

Years later, when Abraham and Isma'il finished building the Ka'ba and going round it seven times, they went to Safa and Marwah and did what Hagar had done. (She had died before Abraham and Isma'il rebuilt the Ka'ba.)

Shaving the head or shortening the hair

'*Umrah* finishes when, after *sa'ī*, male pilgrims shave their heads or shorten their hair, and the husbands or other women cut off an inch or so from the end of the women's hair. After that, the pilgrims can wear their normal clothes again.

Mina

On either the seventh or the eighth of *Dhul Hijja*, the twelfth month of the lunar calendar, all pilgrims have a bath, put *ihrām* on again and go to the hilly valley of Mina some three miles from the Ka'ba. Today Makkah has become so big that one end of the city almost touches Mina and is separated from it only by the hills of Mina. Although there are now some buildings and hotels in Mina, millions will stay in tents. At this time of year, Mina is a city of tents.

Pilgrims wearing ihrām *at Mina*

Arafat

On the ninth day of *Dhul Hijja* all pilgrims go to the plain of Arafat. This is the third obligatory step of *hajj*. It is also the most important part of *hajj*, and pilgrims pour into the field which by this time will have become a tent-city.

A Muslim's experience of Arafat

When I first went there in 1960 I saw the same scene which I have since seen over and over again – the same single-minded devotion, the same praying and walking and the same white-robed souls as if we are all in front of Allah on the Last Day of Judgement. Instead of Allah judging us, we are assessing ourselves, remembering all our sins, promising not to commit them again and praying for His forgiveness. 'Let the judgement, O Allah, be not too heavy on us. Shower Your mercy upon us, O the Merciful, the Compassionate. We all know that we have fallen short of what You expect of us. We have sinned and made our hearts small and selfish. Praise be to You, You have still not taken away Your promise of fulfilment. Forgive us and make us Your true servants.'

I felt as if I had become a guest at a mighty feast and the Great King was bestowing our souls' sustenance upon us all with outstretched hands. For some time I was lifted beyond myself. When I returned a great weight seemed to have been lifted from my soul and I felt free and happy like a chirping bird.

Return to Mina via Muzdalifah

By sunset, caravans and pilgrims on foot move to Muzdalifah, a place between Arafat and Mina. There they say their *maghrib* and *'ishā'* prayers together, collect small pebbles and return to Mina by morning.

Hitting Satan

Having collected their pebbles, the pilgrims then go back to Mina – first to throw pebbles at Satan and then to sacrifice an animal. Both these practices go back to what happened to Abraham and Isma'il:

Pilgrims collecting pebbles at Muzdalifah on their way back to Mina from Arafat

Abraham dreamt that Allah wanted him to sacrifice his most beloved object and later on dreamt that he was sacrificing his son, Isma'il. He went back to Makkah from Canaan. Hagar was still alive at this time. Isma'il was a boy of ten or so. Abraham took Isma'il away and told him his dream. Isma'il told him, 'Father, do as you have been asked to do, you will find me fully co-operative.' Abraham then took him to Mina. On the way Satan tried to dissuade first Isma'il at two places and then Abraham at a third place. But they realised who it was and threw stones at him to drive him away.

Then the moment of the great test came. After Isma'il had lain on the ground and Abraham had covered his eyes with a piece of cloth and was about to cut Isma'il's throat, they heard a voice which they recognised to be from God. It told them that the sacrifice had already been accepted and that a ram had been placed before them. Abraham opened his eyes and saw a ram running down the hill. Father and son caught the ram and sacrificed it. Thus life for life, a ram for the son, became the sacrifice to be performed during *hajj*.

Three pillars have been built at the places where Satan tried to tempt Abraham and Isma'il. Pilgrims commemorate these incidents and hit the first place where this happened by throwing pebbles. On the following two days they hit all the three pillars and thus try to drive away the devil within their own selves.

The sacrifice

Pilgrims also commemorate Abraham's offering of his son's life, the highest example of the submission of humans to the Will of God. On the tenth day of the month of *Dhul Hijja*, many pilgrims offer a sheep or a goat as a sacrifice. It is also an act of thanksgiving to God for His helping them to perform the *hajj*. As pieces of this sacrificial meat are distributed among the poor, the well-to-do learn to share their blessings with the poor and to 'eat of them [the pieces of sacrificial meat] and feed the beggar and the suppliant' (Qur'ān, 22:36).

Shaving the head

After this sacrifice, male pilgrims can again shave their head or shorten their hair and female pilgrims can trim their hair again. This must be done by someone who is not in *ihrām*.

Return to Makkah

The fourth obligatory rite of *hajj*, the final *tawāf* of the Ka'ba in Makkah, can be done after hitting the first Satan. When they have completed this last *tawāf*, the pilgrims become *hājjīs* and *hājjahs* and return home.

Visit to Medina

The Prophet said, 'One who comes for *hajj* and does not visit me is a miser', 'One that comes to my grave and gives me *salām*, I say *salām* to that person in reply', and 'For one that visits me and gives me *salām*, it becomes obligatory for me to pray for God's forgiveness and plead for that person's entry into Heaven.'

Because of what the Prophet said, all *hujjāz* (plural of *hājjī*), especially those from abroad, invariably visit Medina, stand before the Prophet's grave and say 'Peace and blessings of Allah be on you' as if he were alive. They also visit the graveyard of

Medina (Jannatul Baqīyah) and pay *salām* to all the people in their graves. But mostly people like to stay near the Prophet's grave, which is now inside the mosque, because they feel peace and serenity there.

The Prophet's tomb at Medina

THE SIGNIFICANCE OF *HAJJ*

Hajj purifies a person who goes with sincere intention. It also makes the *hujjāz* (pilgrims) feel a kind of unity with all past and present *hujjāz* and a unity with the rest of the Muslim *ummah*. As the black American Muslim Malcolm X said:

> There were then thousands of pilgrims, from all over the world. They were of all colours, from blue-eyed blonds to black-skinned Africans. But we were all participating in the same ritual, displaying a spirit of unity and brotherhood that my experiences in America had led me to believe never could exist between the whites and the non-whites. . . . And in the words and in the actions and in the deeds of the 'white' Muslims, I felt the same sincerity that I felt among the black African Muslims of Nigeria, Sudan and Ghana.
>
> From *Autobiography of Malcolm X*

?

1. Your uncle sends you a ticket to go on the *hajj*. Explain your excitement and the reasons for it in a letter to a friend who knows nothing about Islam.

2. What effect do you think it has on Muslims to feel that they are walking in the steps of the Prophet?

3. How does the *hajj* demonstrate the concept of Islam as one family?

4. a. Imagine that you have made the *hajj* and are staying on in Makkah for a few days. Write a letter to your parents telling them what the experience has meant to you.

   b. Which part or parts of the *hajj* experience do you think you would remember most six months after you had returned home?

Chapter 16

The Islamic Code of Life: Sharī'ah

Islam, as we have seen, is a complete way of life whose foundations are based on certain beliefs (see Chapter 10) and the five pillars (see Chapters 11–15). That complete way of life is governed by a code that Allah sent down for all believers through Prophet Muhammad (pbuh). This code is known as Sharī'ah, the path that leads to God.

Sharī'ah – A Definition

Sharī'ah is the Muslims' complete code of life, derived from the Qur'ān and the Sunnah. It gives all the basic rules and regulations as to how a human being should live and act in political, economic, social, collective and individual spheres, in worshipping God, in dealing with other human beings and in dealing with external nature and natural creatures. To follow it is to become a good human being and to get the blessings of God. To ignore or reject it is to become uncertain, confused and sinful. Sometimes Sharī'ah is also called 'Islamic Law' or 'Divine Law'.

Those who behave according to this all-comprehensive code are known to have behaved morally as well as religiously. Those who do not follow the code are said to have disobeyed God's commands and the Prophet's instructions, and are therefore considered to have been immoral or sinful.

THE SOURCES OF SHARĪ'AH

The sources of this code are the Qur'ān and the Prophet's Sunnah (see p. 50). As the Qur'ān orders all Muslims to follow the Prophet, to follow the Sunnah is to obey God. The Qur'ān touches every aspect of life, but it does not explicitly lay down laws except in some 80 verses dealing with marriage, divorce and inheritance. The Qur'ān was interpreted by the Prophet, who received instructions and guidance from God. That is why the Prophet's practices became the other source of the code.

THE PHILOSOPHY BEHIND THE CODE

A Muslim believes not only that God created human beings, but also that God alone knows what is ultimately good or bad for them. That is why it is for God to tell us what we should or should not do, so that by following God's instructions we may avoid what is wrong and harmful and do what is good and right. Thus a Muslim believes that what is morally right or wrong is what is suitable or unsuitable for human nature.

Faith in this code of life helps a Muslim to follow it unquestioningly. A Muslim does not wait to decide whether the code is good for human beings, he or she follows it straight away. It is only the weakness of their faith that causes many people who claim to be Muslims to be negligent of this code.

Faith, lawfulness and morality are therefore integrated in Sharī'ah.

SHARĪ'AH AND ISLAMIC LAW

How the Code Came to Be Written Down

During the time of the first four Caliphs after the Prophet, there was no written version of a legal system, except for the Qur'ān and Muslims' own knowledge of the sayings and doings of the Prophet. Then, after the Caliphs, the Umayyads ruled (see p. 42), and the application and interpretation of Islamic law was entrusted to the judges (*qāḍīs*). When the Abbasids started ruling after the Umayyads, they encouraged a detailed formulation of Sharī'ah. The most eminent jurists or lawyers of this early period were: Imam Ja'far al-Sadiq, Imam Malik, Imam Abu Hanifa, Imam Shafi'i and Imam Ahmad Ibn Hanbal. Thus five schools of jurisprudence emerged.

These schools of jurisprudence are known as *madhhabs*. A Muslim who follows very strictly one of these schools is said to belong to that particular *madhhab*. Generally, Muslims all over the world stick to one of these *madhhabs* because they find it convenient. It saves them from formulating their own judgements after detailed study of the Qur'ān and Hadīth and anything that the earlier jurists may have said.

Principles to Establish and Expand the Code

The early Muslim jurists formulated three principles from the practice of the Prophet and his companions so that new laws could be made for new situations, which would not contradict the principles drawn from the Qur'ān and the Sunnah. The Arabic legal terms used for these principles are: *ijmā'*, *qiyās* and *ijtihād*.

- **Ijmā'** means the consensus of the learned people (the Muslim *'ulamā*). If, for example, all the elected rulers of a Muslim country passed a law unanimously, but if that law contradicted the Qur'ān and the Sunnah, it would not be regarded as acceptable for Muslims. The *'ulamā* would consider it anti-Sharī'ah.

- **Qiyās** means analogical reasoning. The *'ulamā* are expected to find past analogies for a new situation. This means they find out whether similar situations arose in the past and if so what decisions were taken. Those decisions are then regarded as precedents, and are applied as closely as possible to the new situation.

- **Ijtihād** means the exercise of one's own opinions in questions of law. It means finding out a method suitable for a specific time and place so as to solve new problems in conformity with Divine Law.

Sometimes all these principles are followed, and the range of application of Sharī'ah is extended. For example, certain drugs were declared by the *'ulamā* as forbidden because, like alcohol, they are intoxicants. Similarly, 'test tube' pregnancy has been declared to be permitted as long as it is done with the husband's seed. Surrogate motherhood, on the other hand, is declared forbidden for all Muslims because it is considered the same as adultery.

Al-Azhar University is one of the oldest and most famous universities in the world. It is in the city of Cairo and began taking students in 996CE (386AH). Sharī'ah is a major area of study.

Making lawful things unlawful and vice versa

If God has made something lawful, no human being can declare it as unlawful. Just as no Muslim will accept pig's meat as lawful (see p. 105), eating beef cannot be declared to be unlawful.

Shi'a and Sunni Interpretations

The majority of Muslims are Sunnis, and a large minority are Shi'as. They have the same core of beliefs and practices, but they differ over who can interpret the law. Sunnis believe mainly in four of the schools of jurisprudence mentioned above, namely those established by Imam Malik ('Maliki'), Imam Abu Hanifa ('Hanafi'), Imam Shafi'i ('Shafi'ii') and Imam Ahmad Ibn Hanbal ('Hanbali'). They do not think one can exercise *ijtihād* without first of all trying to find answers in these four schools.

The Shi'as, on the other hand, believe that their acknowledged living religious scholars, known as *mujtahids*, can exercise their own opinions in interpreting Divine Law. No Muslim jurist supports free interpretation of law to suit new circumstances and social change. By *ijtihād* they mean only the attempt to find a method suitable for a specific time and place so as to solve new problems in conformity with Divine Law. Shi'as believe that there was a time when the spiritual leadership of the world was in the hands of the descendants of the Prophet's daughter Fatima and her husband Ali. They are known as *imāms* or leaders. These *imāms*, the Shi'as believe, had the right of exercising *ijtihād* freely.

In the absence of these *imāms*, the *mujtahids* today carry on *ijtihād* as explained above. These *mujtahids* base their opinions on the Qur'ān, Hadīth and the sayings of the *imāms*.

Categories of Obligation

In order to make it easier for the common individual to live correctly as a good Muslim, Muslim jurists have divided things into five categories. They are as follows:

- *fard*: that which is obligatory for Muslims (for example, five daily prayers, fasting during the month of *Ramadān*, and so on),

- *mustahab*: commendable things but not obligatory (for example, praying more than the minimum requirement),

- *makrūh*: that which is detestable but not forbidden (for example, smoking),

- *mubāh*: that which is neither detestable nor commendable,

- *harām*: that which is forbidden (for example, adultery or drinking wine).

These categories, and the distribution of things into them, were not simply made up by the jurists. They were derived from the Qur'ān and the Sunnah. If an issue which did not arise in the early days of Islam has to be decided, certain principles will be used to reach a decision:

- the consensus of the learned and pious scholars of Islam, the *'ulamā*,

- the use of analogy: some similar matter may have been discussed in the past and the decision reached may be relevant to the present problem,

- personal judgement (*ijtihād*), but this is not a licence to do as one pleases. It should only be used when the other two methods result in no clear decision and should be guided by the wish to do Allah's Will.

SHARĪ'AH, ISLAMIC ETHICS AND MORALITY

Ethics is the science of moral duty, of what ought to be. It deals with moral principles, quality or practice, with special reference to a science of ideal human character. Morality is the science or system of morals, in other words the system of what is right in human behaviour. All the ethical systems that philosophers have formulated depend on the concept of what is right or wrong with reference to human nature. These systems are based, therefore, on the philosophers' concepts of human nature and their ideas of what is beneficial and just and what is harmful and unjust for the balanced growth of the human personality. Sharī'ah is a code of ideal human behaviour and conduct, based on the Divine concept of humanity, human nature and the ideal growth and development of the human personality on this earth. We need to know something about that concept of human nature before we can begin to understand why God laid down certain codes of conduct for human beings. The Qur'ān and the Sunnah provide us with that concept and the ideal.

The Qur'ānic Concept of Human Nature

The Qur'ān teaches that two forces combine in a human being, the spiritual and the physical. They are so closely related that it is normally not possible to distinguish between them. They constantly affect one another. They are bound together by a third force, the soul (called *nafs* in Arabic). The spirit of a human being comes from the spirit of God.

Through this spirit Adam was transformed. His personality therefore included qualities such as truth, justice and mercy. God entrusted to Adam the duty and responsibility of preserving all basic values, enshrined in the 99 Names of God, and of making sure that these values flourished on earth. This responsibility has been passed on to the rest of humanity. This explains why every child has a sense of justice, truth, love, kindness, beauty and spiritual values.

However, by coming to earth the spirit has to fulfil physical desires and passions. The spiritual values are ignored or forgotten when a human being becomes the servant of worldly, material desires and becomes a victim of the lowest evil self (al-nafs al-ammārah).

The spiritual self tries to reassert itself in the form of conscience and a struggle takes place. This stage is called the self-in-conflict (al-nafs al-lawwāmah).

Through obedience to God's Will the spiritual self becomes purified and attains peace and contentment. This stage is called al-nafs al-mutma'innah.

Thus the Qur'ān tells us of a dualism which leads to conflict. Sharī'ah shows the way of obedience to the spiritual force. Children have to be initiated into it from an early age so that they will be able to discern it and obey it for themselves as they grow up.

TWO ASPECTS OF SHARĪ'AH

In Islam the responsibility of a human being is divided into two categories: responsibility towards God and responsibility towards the whole of creation. In Arabic, the words huqūqallāh (meaning the rights of God) and huqūq al-'ibād (the rights of humanity) are used to describe these two responsibilities. Thus, for believing Muslims, Sharī'ah emphasises other people's and God's rights upon them rather than their rights upon other people. So far as each individual is concerned, he or she is expected to think more of their responsibilities than of their rights.

These two kinds of responsibilities are not disconnected. God has given instructions to fulfil both of them, and so to fulfil them is to obey God and become a true servant of God. It is in this way that Muslims fulfil the pre-natal commitment to serve God only.

THE IDEAL AND THE PRACTICAL

Sharī'ah thus provides a Muslim with a complete code of life. In the next few chapters we shall see how this ideal is realised in a practical way of life – how a Muslim child grows up as a good Muslim in the family and in the wider community.

?

1 Why would a Muslim argue that it is important to bring up a child with a knowledge of right and wrong from an early age? Why can't children be left to make up their own minds later on?

2 Can you see any link between children learning the Qur'ān by heart and their later behaviour and conduct? Discuss your answer.

<table>
<tr><td>**Chapter**
17</td><td># *The Muslim Community*
and its Festivals</td></tr>
</table>

The Islamic code of life has two aspects in so far as the life of a believer is concerned: the communal and the individual. These are so integrated and arranged that both the community, the Muslim *ummah*, and the individual gain spiritually by doing their collective and individual duties.

THE INDIVIDUAL AND THE COMMUNITY

Every Muslim belongs to the worldwide Muslim community, the *ummah* (see Chapter 8). Politically, economically and socially, each Muslim is held responsible for the good of the community. Sharī'ah lays down the principle that the God-given distinctions of race, colour and language should be accepted as natural. To have prejudice against any particular race or colour or language is anti-Islamic. All conflicts based on such prejudices are condemned in the Qur'ān. The Qur'ān also condemns the uprooting of people from their homes and countries. All countries belong to God and not to any individual or group. This principle applies to Muslims and non-Muslims alike. The Prophet drove out a Jewish tribe only after they had betrayed the trust and conspired against the Muslims after signing the Charter of Medina (see Chapters 4 and 5).

Muslims are thus seen both to belong to the *ummah*, and to have duties towards all the people among whom they are living. A Muslim's neighbours, for example, have their duties towards that Muslim. If a neighbour starves, and the Muslim in the locality does not take note of that suffering and help the person, he or she will be punished by God for having committed a sin. It does not matter whether the neighbour is Muslim or not.

A Sense of Unity

A fellow-feeling or sense of unity is achieved within the community through various means of getting together:

- All Muslims are told by the Prophet that they will get greater spiritual benefit by praying together in the mosques. The mosque becomes a focal point for getting together. The Prophet used his mosque in Medina as his court, his meeting place for all decisions, for education and for prayers. This practice of the Prophet is followed by Muslims throughout the world. All mosques in Britain, for example, are used as Qur'ānic schools for adults and children, for meetings and for festivals.

- We have also seen how Friday congregational prayers bring the whole community together (Chapter 13).

- *Hajj*, as we saw in Chapter 15, is the most successful means of eliminating all barriers of colour, custom and convention that separate different groups.

- The Ka'ba in Makkah is the focal centre of the worldwide Muslim *ummah*. It is the *qiblah* for all prayers, the house that emotionally attracts all believers.

- The Prophet's spiritual presence in Medina is another great source of unity. Hence, like Makkah, Medina has become a unifying place for Muslims.

- Muslims are also united through a common love for God and the Prophet. The Muslim community, as the Prophet said, is 'a single body – when one part of it is afflicted, the other parts feel pain and fever.'

This community is based on the Qur'ān and the Sunnah, and so must follow God's injunctions and the Prophet's example. A Muslim cannot support immoral conduct, injustice, iniquity, communal barbarism, racial prejudices and narrow partialities. The unity of the Muslim community cannot be based on just being Muslim by name. Muslims must also be Muslims in action (*'amal*).

FESTIVALS

Festivals are a manifestation of how the spiritual and moral aspects of human beings are blended with joy and happiness, in which love and respect are generated and maintained.

For Muslims, there are two religiously sanctioned festivals, *'Īd al-Fitr* and *'Īd al-Adhā*, and one socially sanctioned one, *Mīlād al-Nabī*, the birthday celebration of the Prophet.

'Īd celebrations

As well as these three, there are four other occasions which bring Muslims together and inspire them with devotion, charity and love. They are:

- '*Āshūrā*', on the tenth day of the lunar month of *Muharram*,

- *Lailat al-Mi'rāj* (the night of the Ascension of the Prophet to the heavens),

- *Lailat al-Barāt*, on the night of the fifteenth of *Sha'bān*,

- *Lailat al-Qadr* (the Night of Power), which is one of the odd-numbered nights among the last ten days of *Ramadān*, the month of fasting.

Of these the most popular are '*Āshūrā*' and *Lailat al-Barāt*. (As you read the rest of this chapter, you may find it useful to refer back to the Islamic calendar on p. 22.)

'Īd al-Fitr

The month of *Ramadān* ends with the sighting of the new moon, and on the first day of *Shawwāl*, *'Īd al-Fitr* takes place. *'Īd al-Fitr* literally means the Feast of Breaking the *Ramadān* Fast. A short congregational prayer of two *rak'ahs* is said together and a sermon is given by the *imām*. There is no call for prayer. The prayer is a prayer of thanksgiving. Before they pray, the worshippers must give *sadaqah* (alms) to the poor or needy. Both this and the prayer are the expression of the believer's thanks to God for permitting them to fast and receive God's blessings during the month of *Ramadān*.

The prayer-scene is usually grave and peaceful. It is after the *salāh*, the sermon and the *du'ā* to God that the scene changes. Worshippers start embracing each other and even making new acquaintances. In the mosques in Britain, tea, soft drinks and refreshments are served to all.

After that everyone goes home reciting '*Allāhu akbar, Allāhu akbar, lā ilāha illallāhu, Allāhu akbar, Allāhu akbar wa lillāhil hamd*,' which means 'God is great, God is great, there is no god but He; God is great, God is great, all praise belongs to Him.' Those who came to pray also recited this on their way to the mosque or '*Īdgāh* (a place where prayers are held).

The scene at home is equally blissful and happy. Everyone in the house puts on new clothing and eats a sumptuous meal together. In the afternoon or the next day they go out visiting their relatives and friends. Thus *'Īd al-Fitr* becomes a means of strengthening family ties and the ties of friendship, as well as constituting an occasion for the entire local community to get together.

'Īd al-Adhā

Two months after *'Īd al-Fitr* comes the month of *Dhul Hijja*, in which *hajj* takes place (see Chapter 15). All those who do not perform *hajj* pray on the tenth day of *Dhul Hijja* and kill an animal in a ritual way in commemoration of the sacrifice that Abraham made (see p. 82). This sacrifice must be made either on that day or within three days after prayer. It is a symbol of a Muslim's sacrifice of him- or herself to God and is known as *'Īd al-Adhā*.

The sacrificial meat is then divided equally into three portions: one portion for the poor, one for relatives and friends, and one for one's own family. In the East, poor people assemble whenever an animal is ritually killed and their share is distributed immediately. In the West, most of the ritual killings are done with the help of Muslim butchers, and arrangements are made for them to distribute that portion of meat among the poorer people, a large number of whom may be unemployed.

Milād al-Nabī (The Prophet's Birthday)

The celebration of the Prophet's birthday is not a religious obligation, but it has now become a very important socio-religious function of the Muslim community. It has become by far the most important means of reminding both young and old of who the Prophet was, what he was like, what he has done for humankind and what lessons we should learn from him. Through this function, children are reminded every year of the Prophet's greatness, of what he has contributed, of what true Islam is and how one can become a good Muslim.

This occasion is also used to generate love and reverence in the hearts of all Muslims, young and old. It is an occasion to send blessings collectively on the soul of the Prophet. In the Qur'ān, God and the angels are reported to send blessings on the soul of the Prophet, and God asks believers to do the same. By sending blessings on his soul, believers are obeying God and thereby pleasing Him so that they get blessings on themselves in return. This is another reason, and for some the most important reason, why such a celebration should take place.

The Prophet's birthday is celebrated on the twelfth day of *Rabī' al-Awwal*, according to the lunar calendar, which was both the day he was born and the day he departed from the world.

'Āshūrā' (The Tenth Day of the Month of *Muharram*)

At night on the ninth and tenth of *Muharram*, Shi'a Muslims celebrate the martyrdom of Hussain, one of the Prophet's grandsons. This remembrance of Hussain's martyrdom is also important for the Sunnis because Hussain fought against injustice and usurpation. He thus symbolises the spirit of *jihād*, the holy war.

The real meaning and importance of *'Āshūrā'*, however, lies in its being a significant day for all human beings. From the Prophet's sayings we learn that on this day God created the seven heavens, the hills, the mountains, the land and all the seas on this earth. On this day Adam was made and on this day he entered heaven (Eden). Abraham was born on this day and it was on this day that he went to sacrifice Isma'il. Ayyub (Job) was relieved of his sufferings on this day. Jesus was born on this day. This is the day on which Doomsday will take place.

When the Prophet migrated to Medina he found the Jews fasting on this day. On enquiry he learnt that they were fasting as thanksgiving to God for helping them to cross the Red Sea on this day. The Prophet then made it obligatory for all Muslims to fast on the ninth and the tenth. After God's injunction to fast for the whole of the month of *Ramadān* was revealed, however, this fasting became optional. Most Muslims nevertheless fast on these two days.

Lailat al-Mi'rāj

On the night of the Prophet's ascension to the heavens, Muslims gather in mosques to discuss the *mi'rāj* and to pray.

Lailat al-Barāt (The Night of the Decree)

On the night before the fifteenth day of *Sha'bān*, you will see Muslims gathering in mosques, praying throughout the whole of the night or most of it, and visiting the graves of their relations and praying for the good of the departed souls.

Muslims believe that every year on this night God makes his order known to the angels as to who will live and who will die, what will be the means of livelihood of each individual for that year, whose sins are forgiven and who is condemned.

In all Muslim families sweets are made, and chappatis and loaves are either prepared or bought from shops and distributed among the poor. In the Indo-Pak-Bangladesh subcontinent women enjoy making vermicellis, chappatis and *halwā* (sweets) and their labour of love turns the fourteenth and fifteenth of *Sha'bān* into a festive occasion.

At the same time, many Muslims fast for two days – either on the fourteenth and fifteenth or on the fifteenth and sixteenth.

Lailat al-Qadr

On this night, the Night of Power, all devout Muslims try to remain awake the whole night, pray and read the Qur'ān. As it is one of the five odd-numbered nights of the last ten days of the month of *Ramadān*, the devout worshippers try to keep awake on all those nights.

Thus we see how Muslim festivals have deep religious significance. The *'ulamā*, who act as watchdogs of Sharī'ah, always try to keep these festivities within the permitted limits and make believers conscious of any violations.

1   In happy times, Muslims and their non-Muslim neighbours will celebrate festivals together. There are parts, however, which only Muslims can observe. Say what they are and explain why.

2   The Prophet's birthday is becoming a popular festival in Britain. Why? Are there any dangers in observing it?

3   What value do fasts and festivals have? How is the value increased in countries where believers are in a minority?

Chapter 18

The Family in Islam

We have seen how the mosque, the festivals and the Friday congregational prayer are some of the ways in which religious awareness is kept alive in the Muslim community. The Islamic way of life is also fostered and developed through social institutions, especially the home.

Islam regards married family life as the keystone of society and of human social life. It condemns pre-marital and extra-marital sex. Such things are legally punishable offences. Sexual intercourse between unmarried people is punishable by whipping, and adultery by married people is punishable by stoning to death. Free mixing, dating and love-making are therefore forbidden. This does not mean, however, that men and women cannot meet in public or discuss problems or see each other when others are present.

A family at prayer

MARRIAGE

Marriage is part of my Sunnah and whoever disdains my Sunnah is not one of me.

Hadīth

Arranged Marriages

In Islamic society, a marriage arranged by parents or senior relatives in authority is often the most convenient way of getting married. Even when a couple know each other, the process is through negotiation between their parents. Marriage in Islam is such an important event, joining not merely two persons but also two families, that character, piety, intelligence, beauty and wealth of more than one generation are examined.

The views of a British Muslim girl

I do not see why an arranged marriage should not work for me. Though I have grown up in England, I have no objection if my parents arrange my marriage. I know that they will tell me all about the boy and even allow me to get to know him within permitted situations. But I would not want to go out with him, nor would I expect any proposal from him to me. My parents will not take any step without getting my opinion. If I do not approve, they will not arrange that marriage. But I trust them totally.

Free consent of the partners

According to Sharī'ah, both parties must give their free consent. Though it is often difficult to bring the two together so that they can get to know each other better, parents do consult their children and get their opinion before finally deciding.

A young girl opposed her father's choice because the father had not told her anything. They both went to Prophet Muhammad (pbuh). The Prophet heard what both had to say and told the girl, 'You are free to reject, the choice is yours.' She then, on her own, accepted her father's choice.

The Wedding

Except in modern Westernised families, the man and the woman are generally kept apart even during the marriage ceremony. The consent of the bride is sought through witnesses from both sides, who can hear whether the bride says 'yes' or 'no'.

A Muslim wedding

A British Muslim describes the wedding of his niece

British homes are so small! They are not like those in Pakistan, Bangladesh or India, where marriage ceremonies are held in the bride's parents' house. We decided that the best alternative for Shahida's wedding was to have it in the Islamic Cultural Centre at Regent's Park, London. We had to pay to have it there, but it was convenient and seemed appropriate.

We used one room for the women to dress the bride up and keep her there. The men assembled in a large room in the basement. The guests invited by the families of the bridegroom and the bride arrived first. The bridegroom's main party came a bit later. The *Mawlānā* who would conduct the marriage ceremony asked both families to provide a witness. Two people came forward: Shahida's brother on our side, and the bridegroom's cousin on his side. They went to the women's room and asked permission to go in. Strict purdah (seclusion) was not observed, but the women sat around the bride. She was asked three times whether she agreed to this marriage. She said in a very low voice, 'Yes.'

The witnesses then went back like triumphant generals and announced this result to the *Mawlānā*. He asked the bridegroom three times for his consent, not forgetting to mention the amount of money as dowry. The bridegroom was asked first of all in English, then in Urdu and then in Arabic. Poor man! He knew English and Urdu but did not know how to say 'yes' in Arabic. The *Mawlānā* said quietly, 'Say *na'am.*' He did so.

Then the *Mawlānā* recited from the Qur'ān and Hadīth and prayed for the bridegroom and the bride and their future life so that their life may become like the life of the Prophet Muhammad, peace be upon him, and his first wife, Khadijah. We all prayed happily. Someone had brought some dried dates and they were distributed amongst the guests. By now we were all waiting for the last item – a sumptuous dinner with biryani, kebab, paratha and kurma (sweet-meat curry).

After the formal ceremony was over, nearly all the guests left. Then came the women's function, for which relatives had to stay. The bridegroom was taken to the women's section where he had to sit on a decorated carpet by the bride's side. A glass of sherbet was given first to him to drink and then to Shahida. The bridegroom then took a ring out of his pocket and put it on Shahida's ring finger. The ceremony was over. The bridegroom's party took the bride with them to the bridegroom's house.

Husband–Wife Relationship

Mankind, fear your Lord, who created you
of a single soul, and from it created
its mate, and from the pair of them scattered
abroad many men and women; and fear God
by whom you demand one of another,
and the wombs; surely God ever
watches over you.

Qur'ān, 4:1

A wife has the right to be looked after, sheltered, fed and protected. A husband has the right to take the final decisions and to be looked after by his wife. He is head of the family, according to the Qur'ān (4:38). Wives should obey their husbands: 'Righteous women are therefore obedient, guarding the secret for God's guarding' (Qur'ān, 4:38).

Marriage is a contract between two people, but it must be sanctified by prayer. Both the husband and the wife must preserve the sanctity of married life. The Qur'ān regards one as the 'vestment' (clothing) of the other, covering each others' shortcomings in public (2:183). Even sexual intercourse is regarded as a blessing from God. There are religious instructions regarding this, and a prayer which asks for children who will be true servants of God.

> The Prophet once said that a husband is rewarded by God for having sexual intercourse with his wife. When some of his companions were surprised, he said: 'Do you not see that if he were to satisfy his desire in a prohibited manner he would be committing a sin? So if he satisfies it in a lawful manner, he will be recompensed.'

Although the Qur'ān gives a higher social status to the husband, it also insists that the man and woman are partners, that there should be mutual respect, kindness, love, companionship and harmonious living.

> And of His signs
> is that He created for you, of yourselves,
> spouses, that you might repose in them,
> and He has set between you love and mercy.
>
> Qur'ān, 30:20

> It is He who created you out of one living soul,
> and made of him his spouse
> that he might rest in her.
>
> Qur'ān, 7:189

Chastity and modesty are valued very highly in Islam. That is why adultery is punished by stoning to death and sexual intercourse between unmarried people by whipping.

> And approach not fornication;
> surely it is an indecency, and evil as a way [to other evils].
>
> Qur'ān, 17:32

Whom a Muslim Cannot Marry

In Islam there are certain restrictions as to whom you can marry. It is prohibited for women to marry the following:

father, son, brother, grandfather, uncle, nephew, father-in-law, and brother through sucking the same nurse in infancy.

Corresponding female relatives are *harām* (forbidden) for men.

Dowry

Islam makes it obligatory for men to pay a dowry to their wife at the time of marriage.

The Status of the Mother

Although the father is the head of the family, a higher spiritual status is given to the mother. 'At the feet of the mother lies the Heaven of her children,' said the Prophet. He never said the same thing for the father.

Bayazid and his mother

Bayazid was a well-known Muslim saint. After spending many years in meditation and spiritual exploration he returned home and found that his mother had become blind. He then devoted himself to serving his mother. One night she woke up and asked for a glass of water. He brought it to her, but found that she had gone to sleep again. Throughout the rest of the night he stood by her bedside. When his mother woke up and found him waiting for her to call him, she wept and prayed to God. Bayazid used to say later, 'What I earned by waiting by her bedside was more than I had earned spiritually through hard work and meditation during all those years away from home.'

A Wife's Right to Own Property

Islam has given women the right to own property, without obliging them to spend any earnings on the family. Thus, after marriage, a woman may retain her property, spend it as she likes and give it to anyone she likes.

Safeguarding Marriage and Family

Islam tells us that men and women are complementary to one another. It also informs us that, spiritually, morally and intellectually, gender difference is immaterial. A woman can be equally great or even greater than a man. It is only in socio-cultural life that the husband has a higher status than the wife. In the family hierarchy the husband has the highest status, and must be obeyed unless and until he asks for something which is prohibited by Sharī'ah. Husbands must be tolerant and kind – the Prophet said, 'The best of you are those who are best to their wives.' He also said:

> A man is a ruler of his family, and he will be questioned [on the Day of Judgement] about those under his care. A woman is a ruler in the house of her husband and she will be questioned about those under her care.

That is why, to preserve marriage, both men and women are expected in Islam to save themselves from anything that might draw them towards evil.

DIVORCE

'Divorce is the worst permitted thing,' said the Prophet. In earlier religions God did not grant this permission to a married couple. In Islam, however, the husband has the right to pronounce divorce. If he tells his wife 'I divorce you' many times, but in one 'sitting', it is considered to be equal to one pronouncement. This means that he can take back his wife within three months. If he does not do so within this period, the couple has to be publicly remarried.

If, however, the man tells his wife 'I divorce you' deliberately on three separate occasions, then the break-up of the marriage is final. If, after this, the couple want to remarry, they can do so only if the woman has been married to another person and divorced by her second husband.

A wife can also get a divorce from the Islamic court if her husband is sterile or has physical defects or if there are certain other incompatibilities.

As God does not like divorce, He has laid down a process in the Qur'ān of negotiation between the two families in order to bring about a reconciliation between the two.

?

1   Role play a Muslim family discussing an arranged marriage for their son or daughter. What factors do you think that they would take into account?

2   Muslims often live in countries where extended families are more usual than the nuclear families of British society.

   a   Find out what is meant by 'nuclear family' and 'extended family'.

   b   Think of reasons why marriages need to be carefully arranged in extended family situations.

   c   Suggest some difficulties which a husband and wife might experience which could lead to the breakdown of their marriage. Then form groups, and through role play discuss ways in which the extended family might help them. You will need to have at least six members to each group – both sets of parents and the couple. You might add other relatives if you wish. What extra arguments might Muslims put forward against suggestions that the couple might split up?

3   Why do you think the Prophet said: 'At the feet of the mother lies the Heaven of her children'? When you have read the next chapter, discuss what this might mean in the context of child-rearing.

| Chapter 19 | *Growing up in a Muslim Family* |

The Islamic way of life covers everything from birth to death. It includes what food to eat and what not to eat, personal cleanliness, how to greet and treat fellow Muslims, and so on. This chapter begins with the birth of a child and follows it as it grows up in a Muslim family. We see how it learns to eat and drink, how it dresses, how its parents bring it up and teach it manners, rules and regulations, and how it carries out its duties and fulfils its responsibilities.

A group of men and women praying in a family atmosphere

BIRTH

The birth of a child is always considered as a blessing from God. No distinction is drawn between a boy or a girl, but as the family tree is maintained by the boy, couples always like to have at least one boy in the family.

As soon as a child is born, *adhān*, the call for prayer, is recited in its right ear and *iqāmah*, the call to stand up for prayer, is recited in its left ear. The intention is to record in the child's memory cells the basic faith.

BREAST-FEEDING

Breast-feeding by the mother is recommended in the Qur'ān, and is the normal practice in a Muslim family. Two and a half years is laid down as the maximum limit (Qur'ān, 46:14). This is how God wants a loving, intimate relationship to grow between the mother and the child.

'AQĪQAH, OR THE NAMING CEREMONY

Then comes the naming ceremony, which is generally a must in every Muslim house. The ritual killing of an animal is performed as an expression of thanksgiving to God – a goat or a sheep for a daughter, two goats or two sheep for a son. One third of the sacrificial meat is distributed among the poor and one third among relatives, and the rest is usually cooked for family members and guests at the ceremony. Quite often this ceremony is held on the seventh day after the child's birth. The child's head is shaved and the child is brought before everyone present. A prayer is recited for God's help for its future growth, health, prosperity, knowledge and spiritual welfare.

When the companions asked the Prophet: 'O messenger of Allah! We have known the rights of parents but what are the rights of children?' the Prophet replied: 'The father will give a good name and arrange a proper upbringing and education for his children.'

The Prophet also said: 'On the Day of Judgement you will be called by your names and your fathers' names. Therefore keep your good names.'

The choice of a good name is therefore regarded as essential. For boys, the Prophet preferred names that describe them as servants of God. Abdullah (servant of God) or Abdur Rahman (servant of the Merciful) are examples of good Muslim names for boys.

THE BISMILLĀH CEREMONY

As the child grows up, educated parents try to make it learn orally by heart the basic tenets of Islam the *Sūrah Fātiha* (the opening chapter of the Qur'ān) and some other short *surahs* (chapters of the Qur'ān). By the time the child is four or five, a *Bismillāh* ceremony is performed – especially among the non-Arab Asians. A pious or devout senior relative, or sometimes a revered *'ālim* (learned person), is invited to make the child recite the *Sūrah Fātiha* and the first five revealed verses of the Qur'ān, and then to write the Arabic alphabet along with the senior person.

It is a very happy and proud occasion for the child. Dressed in new decorated clothes, with the head covered and a Qur'ān in front of her or him on a *rehl* (a wooden Qur'ān holder), the child is transported to a new world. The function ends with a prayer to God to increase the child's knowledge. Everyone prays: 'O Lord, increase my knowledge,' as the Prophet was taught in the Qur'ān.

QUR'ĀN READING AND SALĀH

Generally, after the *Bismillāh* ceremony is over, the parents teach their child how to do *wudū* (see Chapter 12). They either appoint a *Mawlānā* to teach the child how to read the Qur'ān or take the child to the nearest mosque for evening lessons. Throughout the UK there are many mosques where this supplementary teaching goes on. Generally the *imām* is the teacher. Sometimes, as in Cambridge, a separate Qur'ānic school is set up. The Cambridge Islamic School not only teaches how to recite the Qur'ān correctly, but also teaches Islamic history, rules and regulations of religion and Arabic calligraphy.

Between the ages of seven and ten, a child is expected to learn the five daily prayers

Personal prayer (du'ā') after the Bismillāh *ceremony of Fuad, London*

and to get used to praying regularly every day. In childhood, the child imitates its parents, but after it starts reading the Qur'ān the parents consider it their duty to let the child learn and practise saying *salāh* (the prescribed prayers) on his or her own.

I still remember that when I was six we moved from our village home to Dhaka, the present capital of Bangladesh. My parents, brother and sisters were waiting eagerly in the big boat near our house. I was still reading the Qur'ān and finishing the last chapter. When I completed reading it, the *Mawlānā* who was teaching me caressed me lovingly, raised his hands and prayed.

LEARNING ISLAMIC PHRASES

Throughout its early years, a child learns almost automatically certain Arabic words and phrases, which constantly remind the child of its relationship with God:

● *Bismillāh* ('I begin in the name of God') is a word that the child will hear as soon as the mother starts breast-feeding it. All Muslim children get so accustomed to it that it becomes a habit later on to utter this word whenever the child starts to eat or drink or do any work.

● *Inshā' Allāh* ('If God wills' or 'God willing') is another common phrase that a Muslim always uses whenever he or she talks about the future – 'I shall do it *inshā' Allāh*', 'We shall meet tomorrow *inshā' Allāh*', for example, or 'Will you see me tomorrow?' to which the reply would be '*Inshā' Allāh*'.

● *Māshā' Allāh* ('What God has willed'). Whenever the child achieves something good or great, the parents say automatically, '*Māshā' Allāh*'. The child learns that if God had not willed it he or she would not have succeeded in this way.

- *Allāhu akbar* ('God is great') is a common phrase that the child hears in the *adhān* and in prayers. An idea of God's Might and Greatness is thus imprinted on the heart of the child.

- *Alhamdulillāh* ('Praise be to God') is another very commonly used phrase that is uttered whenever something good happens. All Muslims say this after every meal, and so the child learns the habit.

RULES, REGULATIONS AND MANNERS

Respecting the Family Hierarchy

All are not equal in a Muslim family in so far as duties and respectfulness are concerned. There is a family hierarchy. At the head of it is the father, and then the mother. Then comes the hierarchy of the children. The older one has a duty towards and responsibility for the junior ones. The junior ones must be respectful and obedient to the elder ones.

Greetings and Salutations

From a very early age, the child is taught to say *'assalāmu'alaikum'* to a visitor or when he or she meets a new person or an acquaintance. It means 'peace be with you'. The child says this to its parents before going to bed and when it gets up, and parents do the same. The reply is *'wa'alaikumussalām'*, meaning 'and peace be with you also'. It is more polite and blessed to add to this greeting *'wa rahmatullāhi wa barakātuhu'*, which means 'and on you be the mercy of Allah and His blessings'. This is the usual Muslim way of greeting another Muslim.

The child is also taught the Islamic way of shaking hands. This is done by taking both of the guest's hands into both of your own hands. Men are expected not to shake hands with women, and vice versa, but to exchange greetings.

Visiting a House or Entering Another's Room

By the time a boy or girl is beyond seven, he or she is taught the importance of privacy. Children are taught not to peep into another's room or house, to knock at the door and to enter only if permission is granted. A Muslim is not expected to enter another person's room or house if the reply is in the negative or if there is no reply to the knocks.

Sneezing

Just as a child is taught to get used to saying *'Bismillāh'* before he or she starts to speak or do something, he or she is taught to say *'alhamdulillāh'* (praise be to God) when he or she sneezes. He or she also learns from childhood to reply *'yarhamukumullāh'*, which means 'May Allah have mercy on you.'

Showing Respect to Elders

Muslim children are instructed by God how to show respect to their parents, how to obey them and how not to show annoyance to them – even when they know their parents may be incorrect. They are advised not to argue with their parents. This attitude should also be taken when a young Muslim talks to an elderly person, whether that person is Muslim or non-Muslim.

Showing Respect to Teachers

A teacher should be shown great respect. Once an ordinary person was passing by and the Prophet stood up to show him respect. A companion of the Prophet asked him, 'O Prophet, he is just an ordinary person, why did you show respect to him?' The Prophet replied, 'He taught me something. He is therefore my teacher. I must show respect to him. That is why I stood up.'

That is why it has become good manners among Muslims to show respect by getting up when a teacher enters the room.

Learning How To Be Clean and How To Be Pure

General cleanliness is a characteristic of the Muslim family. 'Purification' is something more than cleanliness. As we saw in Chapter 12, one must do *wudū* or perform *ghusl* as necessary in order to be pure enough to say one's prayers. As the child grows up, he or she learns how to be clean.

The first thing a child learns is how to use a toothpick or toothbrush. The Prophet said, 'The toothstick is a means of cleansing the mouth and is pleasing to the Lord.' The child then learns about washing his or her private parts after using the toilet.

The child also gets used to keeping his or her clothes and body clean and pure. Drops of urine, a dog's saliva, dirt from the street, drops of blood – all these make clothes unclean and impure. They can be purified by washing the unclean parts.

> O you shrouded in your mantle,
> arise, and warn!
> Your Lord magnify
> your robes purify
> and defilement flee!
>
> Qur'ān, 74:1–5

The religion of Islam is clean, hence you should keep yourself clean. No one will be allowed to enter Paradise except he or she who is clean.

Hadīth

Dressing Properly

By the time a child is six or seven years old, it learns to be ashamed of being naked in front of anyone, even its parents. As it grows up, it learns that for boys and men privacy (*'awrah*) is from the navel to the knee, and for girls and women it is the whole body except the face, hands and feet. By the time a girl reaches puberty, it becomes obligatory for her not to go out or be in the presence of outsiders without covering herself properly. Puberty starts when males produce semen and when females start having their monthly periods. Before that time, girls can move about freely, but between the ages of 10 and 14 parents begin to get their daughters used to dressing Islamically. Dressing Islamically means not revealing any part of the body that may arouse sexual passions in men.

> O Prophet, say to your wives and daughters
> and the believing women, that they draw
> their veils close to them [when they go out]
>
> Qur'ān, 33:59

Boys also learn that silk and jewellery are forbidden for them. They are permitted only for girls and women.

The basic principle that Muslim children learn is that clothes must be loose enough to help them do *wudū* and say the prescribed prayers, and to conceal the body in a decent manner so as not to arouse sexual temptation.

No specific dress is prescribed, and this principle allows Muslims to adopt either a traditional local dress or a Western-style long dress with additional *dopatta* or headcover for girls.

Eating *Halāl* Food and Avoiding *Harām* Food

Meat

Children gradually learn what food is permitted (*halāl*) and what is forbidden (*harām*). As they grow up, their parents or the Qur'ānic teacher explain that God has specifically forbidden some kind of food.

> These things only has He forbidden you:
> carrion, blood, the flesh of swine,
> what has been hallowed to other than God.
> Yet whoso is constrained, not desiring
> nor transgressing, no sin shall be on him;
> God is All-forgiving, All-compassionate.
>
> Qur'ān, 2:168

In addition to this, God has also made unlawful the meat of the animal

> strangled, the beast beaten down,
> the beast fallen to death, the beast gored,
> and that devoured by beasts of prey –
> excepting that you have sacrificed duly –
> as also things sacrificed to idols,
> and partition by the divining arrows;
> that is ungodliness.
>
> Qur'ān, 5:4

The Qur'ān also tells believers to 'eat of that [meat] over which God's Name has been mentioned' (6:118) and not to 'eat of that [meat] over which God's Name has not been mentioned: it is ungodliness' (6:121). The flesh of any animal sacrificed to someone other than God is *harām* (forbidden).

The way in which an animal is killed for meat is of the utmost importance in Islam. It is essential that blood is allowed to flow. Research has shown that a sudden blow congeals the blood, and that type of meat is not as good as the meat of an animal that is killed in the way that Muslims and Jews are recommended by God in His message. To kill an animal in the Islamic way, the following things are important:

● the intention to sacrifice in the name of God, saying '*Bismillāh Allāhu Akbar*' (in the name of God, God the Great),

● cutting four arteries of the throat swiftly and with a very sharp knife so that blood comes out profusely and the animal becomes unconscious immediately.

As the Jews also follow this method, their food is *halāl* for Muslims. The Qur'ān says: 'the food of those who were given the Book is permitted to you, and permitted to them is your food' (5:6).

Other foods

Food prepared with lard or cooked with the fat of animals not sacrificed to God – be it biscuits, ice cream, gelatine, steak or oxtail soup – is also forbidden (*harām*) for all Muslims. Muslim parents therefore have to be careful to check the ingredients before they buy food in Britain, or any other non-Muslim country.

Intoxicants (khamr): wine and alcohol

Alcohol and intoxicating drinks and drugs that make people lose their normal sense and weaken their ability to exercise rational judgement are also forbidden (Qur'ān, 5:95; 2:219). Buying and selling wine and alcohol and other such drinks and drugs are therefore sins. Unless absolutely necessary, alcohol should not be used in medicines.

Not Using Gold and Silver Crockery and Cutlery

As children grow up, they are trained by their parents to know that the use of gold and silver cutlery and crockery is strictly forbidden in Islam.

Covering Food

As germs settle on food if it is left open, the Prophet advised Muslims to cover their food and never leave it exposed.

SEX EDUCATION

Sex education must be given to boys by their father or a male teacher, and to girls by their mother or a female teacher. The person who teaches must be a practising Muslim who knows and follows Sharī'ah, and not a person who does not know or does not follow Qur'ānic instructions.

Sex education is given in stages. Between seven and ten, children must learn what is *'awrah* (private) in so far as the body is concerned. They must learn the etiquette of not entering another's room without permission, of not 'looking at' others, and of washing thoroughly after using the toilet.

Between the ages of ten and 14, young Muslims learn what is sexually 'shameful' and 'bad' and that they should keep away from these things. They are also taught not to mix freely with the other sex. Very rarely are girls allowed to go out at night, even for study. Dating is also socially shameful, and the family may be ostracised by the community if this happens.

When males produce semen or have wet dreams and when girls have their monthly period, they are taught to have a bath afterwards so that they can say their prayers.

It is only when they are old enough to get married that they may be taught the science of reproduction and the rules regarding sexual intercourse. There are specific regulations in the Qur'ān and Sunnah regarding them.

It is at this stage that the importance and significance of marriage is emphasised. An aversion towards unlawful sex and adultery is generated in them, and they are given more and more lessons and examples of how a good, happy, peaceful life can be found in married love and a loving family.

PARENT–CHILD RELATIONSHIP

We have charged man, that he be kind to his parents; his mother bore him painfully, and painfully she gave birth to him; his bearing and his weaning are thirty months.

Qur'ān, 46:14

. . . whether one or both of them attains old age with you; say not to them 'Fie' neither chide them, but speak unto them words respectful, and lower to them the wing of humbleness out of mercy and say, 'My Lord, have mercy upon them, as they raised me up when I was little.'

Qur'ān, 17:24–5

Man and young boy wearing the traditional clothes of Saudi Arabia

It is the duty of Muslim parents to bring their children up to become good Muslims. 'Pronounce,' the Prophet said, 'as the first words to your children "there is no god but Allah."' The Qur'ān tells parents to be thankful for God's favour on their own parents and to pray that their seed, their sons and daughters, may also be good Muslims:

> O my Lord, dispose me
> that I may be thankful for Your blessing
> wherewith You have blessed me and my
> father and mother, and that I may do
> righteousness well-pleasing to You;
> and make me righteous also in my seed.
>
> Qur'ān, 46:14

Just as at every stage of their children's development, parents are responsible for their education in etiquette, manners, moral behaviour, moral action and even sexual behaviour, so is it the children's responsibility to look after their parents with reverence and kindness – with *ihsān* (which means kindness, reverence, consideration, patience) – especially in their old age. Thankfulness to God and thankfulness to one's parents are given almost the same status in the Qur'ān:

> Be thankful to Me, and to
> your parents;
>
> Qur'ān, 31:13

Taking care of one's parents is so important in Islam that when a young Muslim wanted to join in a *jihād* the Prophet sent him home saying that as he had an old mother he should look after her: 'Stay with her, for Paradise is at her feet.'

That is why it is forbidden for a Muslim to send his or her parents to an old people's home. The Muslim family thus becomes an extended family, with grandparents playing a full role. They are seen as kind guides to growing children. This has always proved to have a highly beneficial effect on the family. Conflicts between children and their parents are often resolved by the wise care of grandparents.

Wais Karani and His Mother

Wais Karani was a contemporary of the Prophet, a Muslim, a great devotee of the Prophet who loved the Prophet intensely. But he had never seen him. As his mother was blind and he was the only person to look after her, wash her and feed her, he could not leave her to go and meet the Prophet. Once, however, his mother gave him permission to go and see the Prophet. His mother told him to return before sunset. He went to Medina but the Prophet had gone elsewhere. He waited and then had to return home without seeing him. After his mother's death, he went into the jungle to meditate and pray. The Prophet, before he departed from this earth, entrusted one of his cloaks to his close companions 'Umar and 'Ali to be given to Wais. That was Wais Karani's reward.

1 What reasons might a Muslim give for having rules to cover such things as clothing, greetings and crockery?

2 Suggest reasons why Muslims believe that sex education should be given only by people who follow Sharī'ah.

Chapter 20

The Last Rite of Passage

Death is considered in Islam to be the most serious incident in a person's life. Satan is said to try to confuse a dying person and even make that person forget his or her belief in God or have doubts about God and his Prophet. That is why the Prophet advised that relatives should

- be near the dying person,

- recite loudly the *kalimah*: *lā ilāha illallāh* (there is no god but Allah), so that the dying person may also recite this while leaving the world,

- recite verses from the Qur'ān so that the *barakah* (grace) of God may descend and the pains and sufferings of the dying person are reduced,

- pray for the good of the dying person because then, the Prophet said, the angels say 'Amen' to whatever they say.

THE FUNERAL

In many countries we find loud lamentations by women when someone dies. It appears to be a pagan custom. The Prophet forbade it because the departed soul may also feel the pain of the mourners. But sorrow or tears are natural for those who feel the pangs of separation.

Cremation is totally forbidden in Islam. It is believed that the soul feels pain, even though it has been separated from the body, because some attachment still remains. Burial is prescribed – and the sooner, the better.

Before burial the body must be washed and covered in a coffin or a shroud. Washing starts with those parts of the body which are washed when *wudū* is performed. It starts from the right side of the body, and the whole body is washed three, five, seven, or any odd number of times. Washing is performed by people of the same sex.

There are certain rules concerning how the body is covered and how many pieces of cloth are necessary for a man and how many for a woman. When it has been covered, people are allowed to see the face. The body is then carried to a mosque or an open space near a mosque so that people may stand in rows with the dead body in front of them and recite the short prescribed funeral prayer.

After this, the body is taken to the graveyard and slowly lowered down into the grave. It is laid down in such a way that the face is almost turned towards the direction of the house of God, the Ka'ba. Then, leaving an open space in the middle, some wooden planks or stone or concrete slabs are placed on the grave and earth is heaped on top. A short prayer is said, and then friends and relatives depart.

The Taj Mahal, India, built 1632–54. This mausoleum contains the tombs of Mumtaz Mahal and the emperor Shahjahan. It is perhaps the finest example of Islamic architecture.

The bodies of those killed in a *jihād* are not washed. They are shrouded in the condition in which they were killed, and then buried.

The Qur'ān is read at home and, generally on the third day after the death, a prayer is held. On the fortieth day, relatives and friends are invited to read the Qur'ān and when the reading is finished they pray to God to convey the blessings of the reading on the soul of the dead person.

A Supplication of the Prophet for the Dead

O God, forgive him, show him mercy, grant him security, pardon him, grant him a noble provision and a spacious lodging, wash him with water, snow and ice, purify him from sins as You have purified the white garment from filth, give him a better abode in place of his present one, a better family in place of his present one, a better spouse in place of his present one, cause him to enter Paradise and preserve him from the trial in the grave and the punishment in Hell.

AFTER DEATH The Prophet has described what happens to the dying and the dead in the grave. The extract on the next page is a detailed account of what happens after death.

Al-Barā'b 'Āzib said: We went out with the Prophet to the funeral of a man of the Ansari and came to the grave. It had not yet been dug, so God's messenger sat down and we sat down around him quietly. He had in his hand a stick with which he was making marks on the ground. Then he raised his head and said, 'Seek refuge in God from the punishment of the grave,' saying it twice or thrice. He then said, 'When a believer is about to leave the world and go forward to the next world, angels with faces white as the sun come down to him from heaven with one of the shrouds of paradise and some of the perfume of paradise and sit away from him as far as the eyes can see. Then the angel of death comes and sits at his head and says, "Good soul, come out to forgiveness and acceptance from God." It then comes out as a drop flows from a water-skin and he seizes it; and when he does, they do not leave it in his hand for an instant, but take it and place it in that shroud and that perfume, and from it there comes forth a fragrance like that of the sweetest musk found on the face of the earth. They take it up and do not bring it past a company of angels without their asking, "Who is this good soul?" to which they reply, "So and so, the son of so and so," using the best of his names by which people call him on the earth. They then bring him to the lowest heaven and ask that the gate should be opened for him. This is done, and from every heaven its archangels escort him to the next heaven till he is brought to the seventh heaven, and God who is great and glorious says, "Record the book of my servant in *'Illīyun* [the highest Heaven] and take him back to earth, for I created mankind from it, I shall return them into it, and from it I shall bring them forth another time." His soul is then restored to his body, two angels come to him, and making him sit up say to him, "Who is your Lord?" He replies, "My Lord is God." They ask, "What is your religion?" and he replies, "My religion is Islam." They ask, "Who is the man who was sent among you?" and he replies, "He is God's messenger." They ask, "What is your [source of] knowledge?" and he replies, "I have read God's Book, believed in it and declared it to be true." Then one cries from heaven, "My servant has spoken the truth, so spread out carpets from paradise for him, clothe him from paradise, and open a gate for him into paradise." Then some of its joy and fragrance comes to him, his grave is made spacious for him as far as the eye can see, and a man with a beautiful face, beautiful garments and a sweet odour comes to him and says, "Rejoice in what pleases you for this is your day which you have been promised." He asks, "Who are you, for your face is perfectly beautiful and brings good?" He replies, "I am your good deeds." He then says, "My Lord, bring the last hour; my Lord, bring the last hour, so that I may return to my people and my property."

'When an infidel is about to leave the world and proceed to the next world, angels with black faces come down to him from heaven with hair-cloth and sit away from him as far as the eye can see. Then the angel of death comes and sits at his head and says, "Wicked soul, come out to displeasure from God." Then it becomes dissipated in his body, and he draws it out as spit is drawn out from moistened wool. He then seizes it, and when he does so they do not leave it in his hand for an instant, but put it in that hair-cloth and from it there comes forth a stench like the most offensive stench of a corpse found on the face of the earth. They then take it up and do not bring it past a company of angels without their asking, "Who is this wicked soul?" to which they reply, "So and so, the son of so and so," using the worst names he was called in the world. When he is brought to the lowest heaven request is made that the gate be opened for him, but it is not opened for him.' God's messenger then recited, 'The gates of heaven will not be opened for them and they will not enter paradise until a camel can pass through the eye of a needle. God who is great and glorious then says, "Record his book in *Sijjīn* [the lowest hell] and his soul is thrown down." ' (He then recited, 'He who assigns partners to God is as if he had fallen down from heaven and been snatched up by birds, or made to fall by the wind in a place far distant.') 'His soul is then restored to his body, two angels come to him, and making him sit up say to him, "Who is your Lord?" He replies, "Alas, alas, I do not know." Then one cries from heaven, "He has lied, so spread out carpets from hell for him, and open a gate for him into hell." Then some of its heat and hot air comes to him, his grave is made narrow for him so that his ribs are pressed together in it and a man with an ugly face, ugly garments and an offensive odour comes to him and says, "Be grieved with what displeases you, for this is your day which you have been promised." He asks, "Who are you, for your face is most ugly and brings evil?" He replies, "I am your wicked deeds." He then says, "My Lord, do not bring the last hour." '

From Mishkātul Masābīh

---

1   How are people who are dying helped to keep their faith and rely on God?
2   How do the rites which Muslims perform after the funeral help Muslims to cope with bereavement?

Chapter 21

Islamic Ethics

This chapter mentions many things which Muslims must do and some which they should avoid. However, the key principle is sincerity. Outward actions must be accompanied by this inner attitude.

FAITH IN GOD

This is the basis for all goodness. A Muslim, therefore, must be God-conscious and God-fearing. The Qur'ān says that the faithful are those 'who believe, their hearts being at rest in God's remembrance' (13:28) and those who are

> patient men, desirous of the Face of their Lord,
> who perform the prayer, and expend of that
> We have provided them, secretly and in public,
> and who avert evil with good
>
> Qur'ān, 13:22

Such people try to avoid doing wrong. If they should fail, they try to correct their fault immediately. Faith means trusting in the qualities of God and trying to put them into practice. Here Muslims are helped by the Qur'ān and the supreme example of the Prophet Muhammad (pbuh), the perfect Muslim.

MORAL VIRTUES

Truthfulness

As God is Truth, all lovers of God must be truthful. The Qur'ān says: 'O believers, fear God and be with the truthful ones' (9:120).

Love of truth, and hatred of lies, is inherent in every child. A child trusts the person who speaks the truth and dislikes and mistrusts the person who it knows to be telling lies. It is this inherent quality that faith helps to cultivate.

Justice and Fair Play

Just as a little child likes the person who speaks the truth, so it likes the person who is just and fair. The Qur'ān says:

> O believers, be you securers of
> justice, witnesses for God, even though
> it be against yourselves, or your parents
> and kinsmen.
>
> Qur'ān, 4:133

Love of God therefore means love of truth, fair play and justice. The Qur'ān makes this clear:

> whether the man be rich
> or poor; God stands closest to either.
> Then follow not caprice, so as to swerve;
> for if you twist or turn, God is aware of
> the things you do.

> Qur'ān, 4:134

Mercy, Kindness and Compassion

Love of truth and justice does not mean that a Muslim should not be merciful. On the contrary, the supreme example is that of the Prophet himself. The cruelty and barbarism of the Quraysh unbelievers could have been justly punished when the Prophet conquered Makkah. But when they asked for forgiveness, he forgave them all. In other words, he tempered justice with mercy. Allah himself has said, according to a Hadīth, 'My mercy overcomes my anger.'

Compassion should be shown to all, but extra compassion should be shown to the following:

- parents,
- children,
- spouse,
- relatives,
- orphans,
- the sick,
- servants and helpers,
- animals.

When people analyse their own mistakes and the errors, follies, evils, selfishness, narrowness and injustices, however small, which they have done to others, and when they think of the Day of Judgement when they will be in front of God with no one to defend them, then they cannot but become compassionate, merciful and forgiving and give up their pride.

Caring For the Needy, the Poor, the Orphans and the Sick

Allah says in the Qur'ān:

> [The truly virtuous are they who] fulfil their vows, and fear a day whose evil is upon the wing;
> they give food, for the love of Him, to the needy,
> the orphan, the captive [saying in their hearts]:
> 'We feed you only for the Face of God;
> we desire no recompense from you, no
> thankfulness;
> for we fear from our Lord a frowning day,
> inauspicious.'

> Qur'ān, 76:7–10

The Qur'ān is especially keen to make believers conscious of their duty to orphans. That is why, throughout the Muslim world, we find thousands of orphanages. Anyone who can afford to do so, sets up an orphanage, feeds and clothes the orphans and educates them. In Saudi Arabia, the Government takes full care of all orphans, gives them education and trains them to have jobs. The Prophet, himself an orphan, said: 'I and the one who takes responsibility for an orphan, whether of his own kin or of others', will be in Paradise thus' – and he pointed his forefinger and middle finger with a slight space between them.

Orphans are also cared for by the extended family. If the parents die, an uncle will adopt the children into his part of the family. More distant relatives may be adopted in the same way. In one way or another Muslims take great care to ensure the protection of orphans.

Liberality and Generosity

The Prophet was an extremely liberal and generous person. According to Islamic law, as a ruler he was supposed to get one fifth of the booty that was left by the enemies after a *jihād*. Once it so happened that he did not manage to distribute everything that he had got – there were still some goods left over. He did not go home. He stayed inside the mosque. After morning prayer he told his treasurer, Bilal, to see if he could find some needy person. Bilal went out and brought some people among whom he distributed the rest of the goods. That was one of the examples of the Prophet's generosity. The Qur'ān tells believers to give in charity.

The urge to become generous and to exercise charity is balanced by what the Prophet said: 'The best charity is that which is given after you have satisfied your needs.' Abu Salma, on his deathbed, wanted to give all his property to the state. The Prophet did not accept it. He then said he wanted to give half, but again the Prophet did not accept it. When he told the Prophet, 'Then one third,' the Prophet agreed.

Forgiveness

The Qur'ān repeatedly teaches believers to ask for God's forgiveness and to be forgiving oneself. According to the Prophet, the rule is: 'To be forgiving and control yourself in the face of provocation, to give justice to the person who was unfair and unjust to you, to give to someone even though he did not give to you when you were in need and to keep connection with someone who may not have reciprocated your concern.'

Forgiveness thus comes from the generosity which the Prophet asked his companions to cultivate. The Prophet said that the best of people are those who are slow to get angry and quick to forgive. Jealousy, anger and selfishness all prevent us from cultivating the quality of forgiveness. As the Prophet also said, 'Keep away from jealousy because jealousy eats good deeds as fire eats wood.'

Humility

When people experience the loss of loved ones or realise that all that they have – their looks, intelligence or wealth – comes from God, they must be humble. They have nothing to be proud of or boast about. The virtue of humility begins, therefore, with the realisation of dependence on God.

Sincerity

Sincerity is a sign of a good human being. People must try to see whether they are acting to further their own interest in this world or to earn the pleasure of God. If any kind of pride or showing off enters their heart, they know that they have not been sincere. God-fearing people do everything with sincerity, because they do everything for the sake of Allah.

Chastity, Modesty and Purity

Islam asks all believers, male and female, to be chaste in conduct, modest in dress and manners, and pure in intention. Adultery and unlawful sexual intercourse are condemned as heinous sins for which severe punishment is prescribed. People must know how not to be controlled by lust and how to control their sexual passions. That is why marriage is prescribed in Islam.

Patience

Allah tells believers to be patient. The Arabic word used in the Qur'ān is *sabr*, which also means perseverence, fortitude, resolution, self-discipline and control. People must have the strength of mind through their faith in God to control themselves, not be angry or desperate or hopeless, and to resolve to persevere in the path of God against all odds even if it involves suffering. When good fortune comes, people should thank God and not misuse their wealth or waste it or immediately spend it, they should rather persevere to control their desires and use the wealth properly. Wealth is a test of faith and patience.

Brotherliness

The Qur'ān and Hadīth tell us that all believers are brothers. Together they form a single brotherhood that transcends the bonds of race, colour, tribe and language. Common religious practices, a common love for the Holy Prophet and the common cultural code of behaviour draw Muslims together, wherever they may be. That is why the Prophet has said: 'By Him in Whose hand is my soul, a man does not believe until he loves for his brother what he loves for himself.'

The Qur'ān says: 'The believers are indeed brothers; so set things right between your two brothers . . .' (49:10).

Good Relations with People of Other Religions

The Qur'ān tells Muslims to accept all previous prophets as their own, never to criticise any previous prophet or use abusive terms against even the gods and goddesses of other religions (6:108), to invite others to Islam with beautiful speech and 'with wisdom and good admonition' (16:125), and never to use compulsion (2:256). Muslims are instructed to treat others, even if they are non-Muslim, with compassion and justice as human beings.

The Qur'ān tells the Muslims to tell the Jews and the Christians: 'We believe in what has been sent down to us, and what has been sent down to you; our God and your God is One, and to Him we have surrendered' (29:46).

MORAL PROHIBITIONS

Just as God has told the Muslims to be good and to cultivate the virtues mentioned above, so He has also told them to purify their minds and hearts from evils that come from certain activities. In order to be good, a person must know what corrupts the soul and how to avoid these things, to uproot them from the heart and mind. That is why God has told human beings to avoid the following things.

Stealing

Whatever is lawfully earned is regarded in Islam as the personal property of an individual, a family or an organisation. To steal another's things is to break the system approved by God. If a person buys something knowing that it is stolen property, then, as the Prophet says, 'that person is a participant in its sin and its shame'. The punishment for theft, as prescribed in Islam, is the cutting off of the hand. The Qur'ān says:

> And the thief, male and female: cut off the hands
> of both, as a recompense for what they have earned,
> and a punishment exemplary from God; God is
> All-mighty, All-wise.
>
> Qur'ān, 5:42

This punishment, however, is not carried out if there are circumstances that show that the person had no option but to steal, or if there is some *shubhah*. *Shubhah*, in the Islamic legal system, implies that there is doubt about the theft and about the person who has been accused of being the culprit. *Shubhah* also implies extenuating circumstances.

Cheating

Cheating is a form of stealing, and is based on hypocrisy and falsehood. There are several types of cheating:

- giving less than the proper measure or weight,

- hiding the deficiency of goods and selling them as if they were without any defect,

- selling something which is not available, such as fish which has not yet been caught, or fruits or other farm produce before they are ripe,

- going to auctions and bidding for items with the intention not of buying but of raising the price,

- obtaining pre-market information about the price of goods and persuading the seller to sell at a lower price,

- copying other people's answers or answers from a book kept hidden in a desk, or any other unfair means of doing well in an examination and thereby stealing a better place from another student,

- cheating one's employers by not working full time, or by wasting time in non-productive work, but at the same time taking a full salary.

Whatever form it takes, cheating is the product of the desire to gain something without being qualified for it. Faith and fear of God can cure the mind of such false and misleading desires. The best method prescribed by the Prophet and eminent Muslim thinkers is repentance and determination to fight the inner devil.

Gambling

Gambling is prohibited because the winner gets the money without working for it or earning it.

> O believers, wine and arrow-shuffling [gambling],
> idols and divining-arrows are an abomination,
> some of Satan's work; so avoid it; haply
> so you will prosper.
> Satan only desires to precipitate enmity
> and hatred between you in regard to wine
> and arrow-shuffling, and to bar you from
> the remembrance of God, and from prayer.
> Will you then desist?
>
> Qur'ān, 5:93–4

Backbiting

When someone speaks ill of a person who is not present, he or she is said to be backbiting. This is seriously condemned in Islam. Allah says in the Qur'ān that the person who gossips is 'eating the flesh of his dead brother' (49:12). The Prophet said that a backbiter must seek the forgiveness of the person against whom he or she has spoken badly.

People are, however, permitted to discuss the evils of a cruel ruler because only by doing so will others become aware of the ruler's evil ways. Without this, people would be unable to change the ruler or to save themselves from the ruler's sins.

Cursing

Cursing means to abuse someone or to call for misfortune to fall on a person. The Prophet said, 'Do not use bad language, for Allah does not like bad language or the use of it.' He also said, 'The exercise of religious duties will not atone for the fault of an abusive tongue.'

The Prophet also warned, 'Whoever curses a thing when it does not deserve it, causes the curse to return upon himself.'

Suspicion and Spying

> O believers, eschew much suspicion;
> some suspicion is a sin. And do not
> spy, neither backbite one another;
>
> Qur'ān, 49:12

This means that Allah expects people to trust rather than mistrust each other. People should look for faults within themselves rather than find fault with others. That is why it is an evil habit to try to spy on others in order to find fault. Such a person thinks too much of himself or herself. War-time spying on an enemy is not the same thing. In times of war, spying becomes necessary in order to save one's own country. The enemy is always trying to attack. The Prophet himself sent people out to discover what the enemy was planning.

It is spying on other people in order to find fault or do harm that is forbidden. Similarly, it is forbidden to peep into other people's houses – according to Islam, the privacy of other people should be honoured.

Envy

Envy is that evil thing within a human heart which makes a person unhappy when he or she sees someone more beautiful, more healthy, more prosperous or even more generous and better than him- or herself. If we feel envious of other people, we must realise that what other people have are gifts from God, and we should be happy with whatever God has given us. Discontent will only bring unhappiness and destroy our peace of mind. That is why the Prophet said, 'Be on your guard against envying others; for indeed it eats up goodness as fire eats up fuel.'

If people follow God's instructions, they will be able to conquer envy and remove it from their hearts. The Qur'ān says: 'Do not covet that whereby God in bounty has preferred one of you above another' (4:36). If people also remember another of God's instructions they cannot but be happy: 'If you are thankful, surely I will increase you, but if you are thankless, My chastisement is surely terrible' (Qur'ān, 14:7).

The Prophet instructed:

> When one of you sees another who is better off than him in respect of wealth and creation, let him look on one who is below him. That is more proper that you do not hold in contempt the favour of Allah towards you.
>
> Hadīth

Anger

All human beings have anger as one of their passions. But they should not be controlled by anger; they should be able to control it and use their abilities to judge and act soberly.

If anger gets out of control, people lose control over themselves, forget what is right and what is wrong, and may say and do things which, later on, will make them feel guilty and ashamed. Anger makes a person become unjust, behave in an unfair manner, and causes the person to do injustice to his or her own true nature.

Anger can be controlled only when one's love of Truth, Justice and Compassion is strong. That is why the Prophet said a person who is strong and powerful is someone 'who controls himself when angry'. He also said, 'Whoever controls his anger which he has, has the power to show it. Allah will call him on the Day of Resurrection before all creation, and reward him greatly.'

Pride

God alone is the Master, Giver, Sustainer, Destroyer. No one in this creation can be proud. That is why the Qur'ān says that Adam fell because of his weakness. He disobeyed because of his forgetfulness, not because he wanted to be proud. Satan disobeyed because of his pride, thinking he could stand up against God's orders.

> Turn not your cheek away from men in
> scorn, and walk not in the earth exultantly;
> God loves not any man proud and boastful.
> Be modest in your walk, and lower your voice;
> the most hideous of voices is the ass's.
>
> Qur'ān, 31:19

Pride is based on a false idea of possessing something. Proud people may believe that they have made their own beauty or wealth or intellectual ability, and that they will be able to retain and enjoy them forever. But if these people think of accidents or illnesses that may destroy that beauty, wealth and intellectual power, and if they think of death which will come to us all but which may also come without warning, and if these people believe that one day God will judge their activities and see how far they have succeeded in using the powers God has given them, then this pride of possession and selfishness will go.

Only then will proud people cease to mock the less wealthy, the less beautiful and the less intelligent.

SPIRITUAL ATTAINMENT

All the above instructions and prohibitions are meant to purify the souls of people. According to Islam, therefore, the most important thing is to judge whether we are saying or doing anything selfishly or selflessly. This does not mean that one should not work to fulfil one's needs. It means that we should not take any step that makes us selfish, greedy and bad and which forces us to do an immoral thing or something that harms the good of others.

Ideally our intentions should be purified. They can be purified only if our hearts are pure. God tells people in the Qur'ān that in order to be pure we must remember Him always and do everything for the sake of God, and not for selfish goals.

?

1   How do Islamic ethics support the view that values must be based on beliefs?
2   Think of a particular moral weakness. How would a Muslim go about the task of dealing with it?
3   Why might a Muslim say that the greatest *jihād* is the struggle with oneself (the *jihād al-akbar*)?

Chapter 22

Spiritual Enlightenment

Someone may say that they believe in God, know the Qur'ān by heart and live the life of a good, devout Muslim – and they will probably be speaking the truth. But although they have faith, they may lack the deeper, spiritual knowledge of the Unseen which is granted to some people. These are men and women who attain certainty through spiritual experience of God, the angels, Heaven and Hell, creation and the hereafter.

THE SUFIS

Such people are known as Sufis. They follow the path of Sharī'ah, the external legal and moral code of Islam, and also the path of spiritual development known as *tarīqah*. They receive training from spiritual teachers which helps them to follow this path. Sufis are necessary if society is to develop spiritually and become more than a community of law-keepers.

The Beginnings of the Sufi Movement

The earliest companions of the Prophet attained this Knowledge of the Unseen because of the spiritual influence of the Messenger. During the reign of the Umayyads, however, the external legal aspect of Islam became more important than the spiritual aspect. The *qādīs* (judges) who were entrusted with enforcing Sharī'ah did not deal with internal purification – which is the main goal of Islam.

Some companions of the companions of the Prophet, aware of this situation, laid greater stress on methods that would lead people to renounce their worldliness and purify their heart (*qalb*). Hasan al-Basri was one such outstanding person who had both external book-knowledge and spiritual Knowledge. That is how *tarīqah* evolved. It can be said that Sufis have always existed in Islam, but the great Sufi movement began a century or so after the Prophet's lifetime. Some of the most eminent Sufis went to different parts of the world, to preach Islam.

The Difference Between a Sufi and an Ordinary *'Ālim* (Theologian)

The *jihād al-akbar* is common to all Muslims. Sufis proceed through this struggle not only to purify their *qalb*, but to go much deeper, and to acquire more and more knowledge of God, the Prophet, and how God's Will is manifested in creation. The difference between an orthodox *'ālim* (learned theologian) and a Sufi *'ālim* lies in the fact that an orthodox *'ālim* puts the emphasis only on faith. But the Sufi *'ālim* wants also to understand the Unknown and discern what is the greater 'Reality' and what is only relative in this world.

The other difference between orthodox 'ulamā and Sufis concerns the nature of 'ilm (knowledge).

Moses and Khidr

In the Qur'ān there is a story about Moses meeting Khidr. (No one actually knows whether Khidr was a prophet or a saint with extraordinary powers granted by God. But there is a belief among Muslims that he will live until Doomsday, that he is endowed with great power by God, and that he will always help whoever loses their way and invokes his help in the name of God. One spiritual order, the Naqshbandiya order, got special benefit from Khidr because he taught the order's initiator the process of silent remembrance of God through the heart (qalb).)

Moses thought he was the most learned person in the world. God wanted to teach him that he had been granted only one kind of knowledge, the knowledge of Sharī'ah (law). Another kind of knowledge directly from God was granted to Khidr. When Moses went to meet Khidr and spent some time with him, Khidr did things which were apparently against all that Sharī'ah taught. Khidr made a hole in a ferry boat that they had just used instead of giving the ferryman payment, he rebuilt the crumbling walls of a house in a village where the inhabitants were cruel and had refused them food or water, and he killed a child who was standing alone on the street.

When Moses and Khidr were about to part, Moses asked Khidr for an explanation of his behaviour. He explained to Moses that all the things he did were done according to God's pattern, though there was no apparent reason for any of the things he had done. He told Moses that the boatman whose boat he had damaged was a poor man, and he would have lost his only source of income because the ruler of the area was going to confiscate all the good boats.

He then told Moses that he had repaired the wall of the house in the village because it was the home of two orphans, and before their father died he had left two jars full of gold coins for his sons under the wall, and had he not repaired the wall the cruel people of the village would have found the coins and the orphans would have been deprived of what their father had left for them.

He also told Moses that he had killed the child because it would have grown up to be a cruel sinner and unbeliever, and his pious parents would have lost their faith because of their love for their child. Khidr told Moses that they would have another child who would be kind and pious.

The story of Moses and Khidr illustrates how Khidr had been granted another kind of knowledge by God. God had told him to do things that would be beneficial. Although Moses had no insight into what was to happen, Khidr knew what would happen in the future. Khidr thus symbolises the other kind of knowledge that God may grant to some Sufis.

KNOWLEDGE OF GOD

For the Sufi, direct knowledge of God is everything. Once a person knows God, he or she becomes immersed in the love of God and no longer worries about such matters as Heaven or Hell. They also forget themselves, losing things like pride or physical needs for comfort, so great is their love of God.

Self-extinction and Self-purification

This forgetfulness is known as *fanā'*, and it means self-extinction. As a living human being, the person, after such an experience of self-extinction, will of course return to the normal conscious state, but with a difference. The difference is a certainty based on the knowledge of *haqīqah*, which means the Truth or Essence or higher Reality. This knowledge ennobles and enhances the personality, and makes the person indifferent to worldly joy or sorrow. All the moral virtues listed in Chapter 21 become part and parcel of that person's being.

Someone who has acquired this knowledge and who has passed through the stages of self-extinction and self-purification is a Sufi. Someone who is initiated into the path of *tarīqah* is known as a *murīd*.

SILSILAH (SPIRITUAL LINEAGE AND ORDERS)

All Sufis claim a direct relationship with the Prophet, and trace their spiritual lineage back to the Prophet's companions and through them to the Prophet himself. This spiritual lineage is known as *silsilah*. It also means an order to which people following a Shaykh (a Sufi teacher) belong. Quite often each order has a head through whom the entire order remains united in a brotherhood. Before his death, a Shaykh generally appoints a successor. All *murīds* must show total obedience to their Shaykh and to their order.

As *tarīqah* is spiritual training, the knowledge, technique, method and energy are all internal and spiritual, and cannot be understood simply by reading about them. The Shaykhs claim that they have learned *tarīqah* from their Shaykhs, who ultimately derived it from the Prophet, through his companions.

A Shaykh, Egypt

Most of the *silsilahs* go back to the Prophet through his son-in-law 'Ali, who was the fourth Caliph after the Prophet. Three well-known *silsilahs* are Qadiriya, Chistiya and Suhrawardiya. Another well-known *silsilah* is Naqshbandiya, which goes back to the Prophet through the first Caliph, Abu Bakr.

KHĀNQAHS OR ZĀWIAHS

A *khānqah* or a *zāwiah* is a place where Shaykhs meditate and remember God and train disciples in the spiritual path. Throughout Muslim history, these places have been great centres of religious learning, spiritual activity, and moral reform and advancement. They also acted as centres of Muslim missionary work. Later on they became shrines where the Shaykhs were buried. Even today, they are visited by thousands of Muslims. Ayubia, in Istanbul, where a famous companion and relative of the Prophet lies buried, is one such place.

Some of the most well-known shrines, which are also thriving centres of spiritual and religious activity, are: the shrine of Shaykh Abdul Qadir Jilani in Baghdad, in Iraq, the shrine of Shaykh Muinuddin Chisti in Ajmeer, in India, the shrines of Shaykh Shah Ali in Dhaka and Shaykh Shah Jalal in Sylhet, both in Bangladesh.

THE ROLE OF THE SUFIS

In the past, Sufis played a great role in many ways. They continue to play an important role today.

- They saved Islam from being turned into just an external legal code, observance of which was often held by a section of Muslim jurists as enough for salvation.

- They fought against those philosophers who tried to turn God into an inert principle of metaphysics.

The shrine of Shaykh Muinuddin Chisti in Ajmeer, India

- They have kept alive the basis of *īmān* (faith) which, as the Qur'ān and the Hadīth say, is love for God and the Prophet.

- Because of their own humility, sincerity and devotion, and the way they have become examples of virtue in their character and conduct, they have had a great impact on people. Through them, millions of non-Muslims accepted Islam in different parts of the world.

- They have produced great classics of literature in different languages, especially Arabic, Persian and Urdu. One of the greatest mystical poets of the world was Jalaluddin Rumi, whose *Mathnavī*, written in Persian, is a monument of unique beauty and grandeur.

- Sufism gave birth to great intellectual activity; great Sufis have produced works on theology, philosophy, politics and ethics.

- Sufis play a very great role in keeping Islam alive today. They kept Islam alive in Turkey after Turkey was modernised by its dictator Kemal Ataturk when he seized power after the First World War. It was Sufis who kept Islam alive in the hearts of people during the campaign of Communist Russia to destroy the spiritual and religious aspects of Islam.

SUFIS IN THE MODERN WORLD

Wherever and whenever the threat of worldliness endangers Islam, the witness of the Sufis will be needed to counter materialism. Sufis have an important part to play when religion becomes a matter of rule-keeping rather than an affair of the heart. Many Muslims would feel that they are needed as much in the modern world as they were centuries ago – perhaps even more.

1   How did Khidr teach Moses that there is more to life than what appears on the surface?

2   Spiritual pride is always a danger for Sufis. Why? How can they avoid it?

3   Why have (a) some Muslim rulers and (b) some theologians been suspicious of Sufis?

4   Try to find out something about the work of a particular Sufi.

Chapter 23

Muslims in Britain

Muslims form the largest religious minority in Britain. There are no accurate figures available, but from different sources it is estimated that the total population of Muslims, including children, is probably more than a million.

Before the Second World War, there was only a tiny minority of Muslims in Britain, and they were mainly confined to London, Glasgow and some other ports. Their presence was made known to the public by the Woking mosque, which was set up in 1889, and later on by the Aldgate East London mosque, which was built after the First World War.

After the Second World War, when there was an increased need for cheap unskilled labour, the British authorities drew on the Commonwealth for the people they needed. The result was a sudden on-rush of male Pakistanis, Indians and Bengalis. The pre-partition killings in the Punjab and Bengal also led many people to come to Britain and, in 1971, there was another rush of immigrants from East Pakistan (now Bangladesh), because of the civil war there. In 1961, the British Government allowed all Commonwealth people to opt for British nationality. Many did, but some did not.

Although at first it was mainly men who came, later on they were allowed to bring their wives and children. They in turn persuaded other relatives to come and get jobs. At first money was the sole attraction, and coming to Britain was not seen as seeking a place for permanent settlement. But as their families and relatives arrived, and they began, to some extent, to feel a traditional home atmosphere, they did not return 'home' as originally intended, except to visit once every one or two years. Most of them had an idea of returning home eventually, as many still do today, and for this reason they sent money back to their country of origin, bought land and property and built houses 'at home', ready for their return. Some workers have now returned home, transferring the pension rights which they gained from their employment in Britain, to their 'home' country's currency, which allows them to live there in comfort. The second and third generation Muslims, however, especially those who were born and brought up in Britain and have learnt to speak English, feel hardly any attraction to what their parents call 'home'.

Composition

This community is officially bracketed with other communities of Asian origin, and the people are 'branded' as Asians. But in fact the British Muslim community is more varied than this label implies. It consists mainly of people of Bangladeshi, Pakistani, Indian, Turkish, Arab, Iranian and British origin. It also includes a large section of Arabs of Egyptian, Sudanese, Algerian, Libyan and Tunisian origin, as well as a number of others of Palestinian, Jordanian, Syrian and Iraqi origin. Finally, there are Nigerians and others of African origin who also form part of the British Muslim community.

One way to find out just how varied this community is is to go to the Central London mosque in Regent's Park and see who attends the Friday prayer and 'Id prayers. You will find many of them dressed in colourful national clothes.

Since so many of the first group of Muslims to come to Britain were male, at first there was an imbalance between the sexes. Now, however, there is more of a balance between the numbers of men and women in the community.

The tightening of the immigration laws has made it difficult now for large numbers to come to Britain to settle down permanently. Nevertheless, there is still a constant trickle of Muslims arriving from different parts of the world. There is also a small but growing number of native British people who have converted to Islam and become Muslim. Intermarriage between native British converts and Muslims of Asian or African origin is a happy sign of intermixture.

Identity

The British Muslim community has two characteristics so far as identity is concerned. They are one and united in their feelings when a common cause is at stake. This oneness they feel with all other Muslims in the world at large. At the same time they belong to different local traditions, and speak of different group interests, identifying themselves as Bengali or Pakistani or Egyptian or Iranian. Different languages keep alive these differences and they have their own organisations looking after their separate interests. Only when the children and grandchildren of the first Muslims to come to Britain have grown up knowing only English, unfamiliar with their country of origin, will the Muslims in Britain identify themselves simply as British Muslims.

This will not be achieved very easily, however, because of the different organisations with their origins in India, Pakistan, Bangladesh and Egypt, for example, which are keeping alive their non-British identity. The first generation of immigrants have not shed their sense of belonging to places outside Britain, although the second generation has started talking of Britain as their own country. The fragmentation that has been noticeable among British Muslims will be removed only when the new generations start participating fully in local activities.

MUSLIM AND BRITISH CULTURES

Little thought was given to the migration of large groups of Muslims to Britain, any more than had been given to Jewish, Irish or east European people who came to Britain earlier in the twentieth century. The authorities expected that they would merge into British society, that they would be assimilated. This did not happen.

Neither did the Muslims in Britain become integrated into the main cultural stream. The authorities, as the Muslims, now feel that the way forward is some form of pluralism in which the Muslims accept a common framework of overarching values such as the English language, justice, democracy, and at the same time retain their

A house-mosque in a British Muslim home

own religious values. Muslims are working out what it means to be Muslim and British, and Britain is adjusting to being a multi-cultural, multi-faith society.

In the remaining pages of this chapter we shall look at some of the issues which Muslims and non-Muslims might consider. First, however, we must pay attention to the main cause for Muslim anxiety.

Values and Practices: Tension and Conflict

There are many aspects of British society which Muslims cannot accept because Islam condemns them. Muslims fear that their children will be influenced by them. The most significant of these are:

- the stress on individual liberty which often clashes with the Islamic importance of the family and community. Muslims worry that their children may go their own way, neglect their parents in their old age, marry partners who are not Muslims,

- the emphasis on sex and sexual freedom. The social mixing of men and women outside the family is unacceptable to many Muslims. Sexual intercourse must take place only within marriage. Clearly these two principles conflict with such things as co-educational secondary schools and colleges, mixed wards in hospitals, patients being seen by doctors of the opposite sex, and a whole 'pop' culture which seems to take sexual freedom and homosexuality for granted. In Muslim countries sex is not used in advertisements to sell coffee, cars or anything else. Muslims are surprised and disturbed by many of the advertisements which surround them as well as by the culture which they reflect.

Sources of Tension and Conflict

Islam is a total lifestyle. Compromise on the things which Muslims consider true is impossible. In certain matters Muslims also feel that the dominant British culture is attempting to impose its practices. The result is often conflict. Below we look at some particular issues which have been the source of conflict.

Halāl *food*

Meat from an animal which has been killed according to Islamic tradition is not always available in British schools or hospitals. This compels Muslims to eat only vegetables or eat the meat which Muslim canteens provide. As tax payers, Muslims believe that their requirements should be met.

Clothing

There has been conflict over the clothes worn by Muslim girls in secondary schools. In one case, two sisters decided to go to school wearing long dresses and covering their heads. The head teacher did not allow them to stay. The girls returned home, but went back to school every day dressed in the same way, since that is what Islamic law demands. Finally the school governors allowed it, on condition that the colour of the girls' clothes should be that of the school uniform. Both parents and children accepted this regulation.

According to Sharī'ah or Islamic law, Muslim girls cannot wear short games clothes or swimming costumes. Mixed swimming, or swimming by girls which is open for the other sex to see, is strictly forbidden in Islam. Muslim girls cannot therefore join school swimming lessons or participate in mixed games.

Privacy is another regulation strictly followed in Muslim houses. Grown up girls and boys cannot be seen naked, even within their own sex group. Muslim parents therefore demand privacy for their children at school for taking showers or changing clothes. Most school authorities even now do not understand the Islamic injunction, and are not ready to provide the necessary facilities.

British Muslim schoolgirl

Sex education in schools

Sex education in particular, and the open manner in which it is pursued in many British schools, is the cause of a huge tension in the British Muslim community. According to Islam, sex education showing the reproductive organs and discussing sexual intercourse, is forbidden. Presenting the idea of 'safe sex' with the help of contraceptives is also forbidden. Sexual intercourse outside marriage is a punishable offence in Islam, and masturbation and homosexuality are sinful and considered physically and emotionally harmful. Islam considers the presentation of sex clinically through science in biology classes to be undesirable and wrong. In personal relationships, sex should be presented as something which leads to happiness within stable married life, and which is permitted only within married life so that both partners feel emotionally, morally and legally committed. But in British schools, sex education has become cross-curricular, thus making it extremely difficult for Muslims to withdraw from sex education classes. As a result, tension and ill feeling is created within the Muslim community.

The Islamic Academy in Cambridge, set up by Muslims and working in close collaboration with the Department of Education of Cambridge University, realises that this tension exists in the Jewish, Christian, Hindu, Buddhist and Sikh communities as well. It therefore arranged a seminar at which representatives of these religions discussed the matter and openly challenged those school authorities which are not following the official circular advising schools to teach sex education within the context of stable married life. In cooperation with other religious groups, British Muslims are now carrying out a campaign throughout the country.

Possibly the main reason why these problems are not more easily resolved is that the parents of many of the Muslim schoolchildren do not understand English and do not, therefore, go to the schools to make their grievances known. Some schools do provide interpreters, but most do not and as a result there is no mutual understanding between the schools and the Muslim parents. The problems then take on a political colour when the parents go to the local Muslim organisations.

MUSLIM WOMEN IN BRITAIN

Islam gives a Muslim woman rights to choose her partner, own her property even after marriage, receive a dowry, and have a high status as a wife and mother. She is also expected to obey her husband. Although arranged marriage is the general practice, most of the young Muslim girls in Britain are much freer than their friends in the more orthodox Muslim world, and their parents are realising this. Some girls are influenced by the mixed society and their white peer groups, and also by those elements in their own community who try to mislead girls.

Women are also keen to make a career. They study. Whereas previously most Muslim parents liked their sons to study while their daughters completed their education and married – if they could arrange marriages. More parents now have no objection if their daughters decide to follow a career.

SOME MUSLIM RESPONSES

Organisations

Because of such tension in the British Muslim community, several international organisations, and a number of new smaller organisations, are working in Britain to keep young Muslims on the right path. The Tabligh movement is one of the leading international organisations. They have their headquarters in Dewsbury. Missionaries go from door to door, talking to Muslims in order to instil new energy into them so that they may not fail or falter. Several Islamic youth organisations have been set up and a central body, FOSIS (Federation of Students' Islamic Societies), started working in 1963. It organises a large annual gathering to reinforce orthodox Islam. Some of these organisations produce news sheets, bulletins and papers, and are deeply engaged in keeping alive the orthodox tradition of Islam.

The Muslim Institute of London works to preserve Muslim identity by following a policy of exclusiveness and segregation. This is a political move, and an Islamic political party has already been launched. At its forefront are native British Muslims. At the same time, some educated Muslims have joined British political parties and are becoming mayors and local county councillors. They want to retain the interest and culture of the Muslims, and to achieve this through cooperation, not through confrontation.

Muslim Education

Already there are signs that the age-old customs of Islamic society will not be overthrown completely. Rather, they are being reinforced through supplementary schools which teach children how to read the Qur'ān, how to say their prayers, and how to fast. These schools are held after normal school hours. Those who can afford it, appoint *Mawlānās* (teachers) to come to their homes and teach the children.

In some of these supplementary schools, such as the one in Small Heath, Birmingham, children are taught to learn the Qur'ān by heart and to become *huffāz* (pl. of *hāfiz*, memorisers of the Qur'ān). In Dewsbury and Coventry, there are traditional theological institutions, known as *madrasahs*, where Islamic theology is taught and students get degrees to enable them to teach Islam and Islamic history and culture.

Muslim schools in Britain

Muslims in Britain are currently trying to set up independent single-sex schools and to get voluntary-aided status for them. As sexual morality is highly prized in Islam, and is tied up with the honour of the family as a whole, and as free mixing in schools and in the surrounding ethos of non-Muslim white society provides too many temptations for young Muslims to break away from the religious tradition of the family, Muslims have launched a movement and have already set up several schools. Mr Yusuf Islam's Islamia school and a girls' school in Bradford are well known. The Saudi Arabian Government has set up a school for the children of Arab and other Muslim consulate and embassy staff. A similar school for boys, known as Darul Uloom Islamia school, is functioning in Birmingham. The Small Heath school in Birmingham, consisting of nearly 80 per cent Muslim children, has opted out of local education authority control. Yusuf Islam's Islamia school has applied for voluntary-aided status. These indicate a growing need for single-sex schools controlled by Muslims.

The work of the Islamic Academy (see p. 129) indicates a far deeper need by the Muslim community as a whole to meet the challenge of the secularist philosophy and the secularisation of every branch of life including religion. In view of the fact that Christians are cooperating with this move, it may have a far-reaching effect and stem the tide of secularisation of the Muslim community, thus enabling it to retain its total Islamic character.

?

1   Record on video a group of TV advertisements one evening. Would any of them be unacceptable to Muslims? If so, why? (You could look at advertisements in some magazines in the same way.)

2   How might a Muslim politely reply to school governors who turned down a request for *halāl* meat to be served in school meals?

3   If you were a non-Muslim and went to live in a Muslim country, what aspects of your way of life would you expect to keep? Which would you be prepared to give up? Give your reasons.

4   If you were a Muslim living in Britain, would you send your children to a Muslim school if one was available? Give reasons for your decision.

Chapter 24

Conclusion:
Islam in the World Today

Nearly all the Muslim majority countries (see the map on p. 1) were under European imperialist powers till the end of the Second World War. By the 1960s, they had become independent national states. They still feel that they belong to one common Muslim *ummah* (community). That is why most of these states got together in 1969 and set up the Organisation of Islamic Conference (OIC) which arranges annual meetings of the foreign ministers of these states. The OIC has divided the Muslim countries into three groups: the Arab states, the African states and the Asian states.

As well as this feeling of belonging to a common Muslim community, these states also exhibit a sense of unity with other groups: the African states belong to the Organisation of African Unity (OAU); Pakistan and Bangladesh belong to the South Asia Association for Regional Cooperation (SAARC), along with some non-Muslim countries and also to the British Commonwealth of Nations.

**THE INFLUENCE
OF THE WEST**

The effects of western domination can be seen in the political, economic and cultural life of the Muslim countries.

The Political Field

Muslim majority countries today have various forms of government, ranging from some form of democracy to military dictatorships and hereditary monarchy. The Caliphate (which started after the Prophet and ended with the last head of the Ottoman Empire, Abdul Hamid) was abolished by the military dictator of Turkey, Kemal Ataturk, in 1924.

No Muslim country follows Islamic law (Sharī'ah) as its entire legal system, though Saudi Arabia follows the criminal law of Sharī'ah. When the western powers were in control of these countries, they installed their own legal system; they allowed Islamic law to be exercised only in some personal matters. Turkey chose to adopt the western legal system. In Iran, after Ayatullah Khomeini overthrew the Shah, the new government started trying to change the entire system and make it Islamic. A new kind of democracy is now established in Iran which combines western democratic methods of election with Islamic rules and regulations.

The Economic Field

Economically, the Muslim countries are in the grip of the western capitalist system in which interest (*ribā*) plays a key role. Interest is forbidden in Islam. But as the world economy is governed by the western system, the Muslim countries cannot implement an interest-free system unless they try to do it collectively. Interest-free Islamic Banks have been set up as private enterprises by some Muslim entrepreneurs, but as yet no comprehensive interest-free economic theory has been fully formulated. Islamic economics is now a subject of teaching and intensive research.

The Cultural Field

Culturally, the modern western secular education system has brought secularism to Muslim countries. People in the West, including Jews and Christians, have become used to dividing their knowledge and their activities into two sectors: the secular, this-worldly sector and the Divine, other-worldly spiritual sector. Political, economic and social theory and activity are considered this-worldly affairs and they need not depend on concepts drawn from religion. If anyone gives a religious view, it is seen as one of many approaches. For Muslims, however, all activities and approaches are governed by the ideas and concepts found in the Qur'ān and the Sunnah. For all activities, Muslims seek guidance from the way the Prophet applied the Qur'ān in daily life.

Modern secular education teaches only western ideas about society, external nature and human beings. Philosophy, psychology, sociology, political science, economics – all these are taught according to theories and concepts which have nothing to do with Islamic ideas of human beings and nature. As a result of this influence, there are now some people in the Muslim countries who want to turn religion into something which is purely personal and private, and to follow the western ways in political, economic and social life: this-worldly life. The Muslim *ulamā* (scholars) and those who want to preserve and propagate Islam in its true form are therefore in conflict with those who want to follow the western pattern. Thus there is a tension in all the Muslim countries.

Where Muslims are in the minority, especially in the West, many Muslims face a similar tension in their own lives. Whilst not wanting to put up a barrier to knowledge, they believe they must continue to live and think Islamically. How can they do so when they are living in the West? How can they do so without meeting the challenge of scientific theories such as the 'theory of evolution', which contradict the Islamic theories about creation and human nature? They cannot change the Islamic code of morality and man–woman relationships, so how can they live in a modern western society which is influenced by non-Islamic codes and ideas about sex-relationships?

THE ISLAMIC RESPONSE

The traditional *ulamā* were unable to answer these questions. In the nineteenth century, they tried to preserve Islam by preaching seclusion. A small group tried to compromise with modern science and reinterpret the Qur'ān from the point of view of modern scientific theories. But this compromise was not satisfactory and people did not accept it.

In the twentieth century, a new group of Muslim scholars, theorists and organisers have emerged. They are well-versed in modern life and values and are also learned in Islamic thought. They have provided new answers to the questions, especially on the political front and in education, and have taken some practical steps.

A New Political Ideology

Several new Islamic political-cum-cultural organisations and leaders have sprung up. Some of the more important of these are:

- Hasan al-Banna set up Ikhwanul Muslimeen (Muslim Brotherhood), whose intellectual spokesman was Syed Qutb. Its influence is widespread throughout the Arab world.

- Maulana Abul Ala Mawdudi set up Jamaat-i-Islami, which operates in Pakistan, India and Bangladesh. Its theorist was Maulana Mawdudi himself.

- ABIM was set up in Malaysia. It is the most influential organisation among young Muslims both politically and intellectually.

- Dr Muhammad Natsir, who was the first prime minister of independent Indonesia, is still the most influential Islamic force in Indonesian Muslim culture.

- The most practically successful authority was Ayatullah Khomeini in Iran, whose book *Vilāyat-e-Faqīh* suggests the new way of running a Muslim state.

The most important idea they preached was that only with a genuine Islamic authority in power can Muslims retain, preserve and propagate Islam; have an opportunity of replying to western secularist thought in theory and in practice; and succeed in proving to the world that the Islamic alternative is the only correct process for humanity, if humanity is to be saved from moral degeneration and total destruction.

The common elements in the theories of these organisations and political movements are:

- The assertion that sovereignty belongs to God alone.

- The Qur'ān and the Sunnah are the basis of the entire legal structure, and no law shall be passed that would be contrary to these two authorities.

- Freedom and justice for all are ensured.

- Law-making authorities should be elected, but there should be a law-validating body through election or selection from the existing 'ulamā of the land.

- The executive authority must be an elected body or a person selected from among the most pious and righteous of the country. According to Ayatullah Khomeini the authority should be a jurist (*faqīh*). The process of election may vary.

- Dictatorships or hereditary kingships are not regarded as Islamic in origin.

- There must be peace among Muslim groups and among Muslim and non-Muslim groups.

- *Jihād* is obligatory for all Muslims when they are wrongly attacked or when Islam is under threat.

- Private ownership is permitted along with public ownership and state ownership.

- Wealth is a trust and a gift from God, hence poor people have rights over that wealth – rights to be fulfilled by the wealthy through obligatory 'poor due' (*zakāh*), through personal, voluntary, charity (*sadaqah*), in the form of donations to charities, organisations or individuals, and through the equitable distribution of wealth.

- Charging interest (*ribā*) on loans and hoarding are sins and hence forbidden.

- Equitable distribution of wealth is ensured through the law of inheritance and through other means prescribed in the Qur'ān and the Hadīth.

- Wealth must be utilised for the welfare of the people in order that 'it [wealth] be not a thing taken in turns among the rich of you' (Qur'ān, 59:7).

A New Educational Movement

Education, the most important means of transmitting Islamic culture, is also the most powerful means of secularising the minds of children. An Islamic educational movement was therefore set up in 1977 as a result of the First World Conference on Muslim education in Makkah. The intention was to counteract the influence of secularist thought and to provide educationalists with a viable faith-based alternative. This conference was followed by four other conferences in Islamabad (1980), Dhaka (1981), Jakarta (1982) and Cairo (1987). They have succeeded in providing an Islamic philosophy of education, based on the concept of the balanced growth of the total personality through the cultivation of faith in fundamental qualities such as justice, truth, mercy, love and charity implanted by God within every human soul. They have also begun to replace basic western concepts with concepts drawn from religious ideas of human nature.

New curricula and teaching methodology based on these concepts are now being worked out and tried in Muslim schools in Britain and America. The impact of the conferences and the work resulting from them is gradually being felt both in Britain and America and in some Muslim majority countries. In England, the Islamic Academy of Cambridge is trying to get the assistance of other religious groups in order to press for this new religious alternative to be recognised as a valid approach. Among the Muslim countries, the Malaysian government has decided to overhaul their secularised education system. There is a growing recognition that the conflict in the Muslim community between those who are educated according to the traditional religious schools without modern knowledge and those who are educated in the western secular system without adequate knowledge of Islam can only be solved if this new education system is adopted – especially in the Muslim countries.

Muslims in Britain: New Political Activity

Muslims in Britain are already playing their part in the politics of the country. There are three different trends in the political activity of British Muslims:

- To join the existing political parties, stand for election to county councils, city councils and parliament, and thereby stress the Muslim presence and preserve the Muslim identity. Already there are Muslims who serve at city and county council levels and several Muslims have become mayors, but there are not yet any Muslim Members of Parliament.

- To form a purely Islamic political party, exclusively Muslim. Native British Muslims have already launched the Islamic Political Party.

- To create exclusive political consciousness by establishing a 'Muslim Parliament' where continuous assessment of the existing political work by the parties shall be made and the Muslim viewpoint shall be recognised, expressed and publicised. This is the proposal of the Muslim Institute of London.

GLOBAL IMPORTANCE OF MUSLIM POLITICAL PRESENCE

The discovery of oil in the Middle East, especially in Saudi Arabia, the Gulf areas and Iran, and the utilisation of the oil money to educate children, set up industries, develop agricultural products and, at the same time, support other Muslim countries have regenerated the Muslim world. The newly awakened Muslim youth aspire to be the most advanced in knowledge and practice and the staunchest followers of the Qur'ān and the Prophet. This is especially true of a large number of students who were born and brought up in western countries and of those who support the Muslim Brotherhood and Jamaat-i-Islami. The Muslim Students' Association of the USA (MSA) and the Federation of Students' Islamic Societies (FOSIS) of Britain also reflect this new attitude. Salman Rushdie's satirisation of Islam, the Prophet and his family in his book *The Satanic Verses* brought together diverse Muslim groups to protest about the book. This gave a new impetus to establish, preserve and maintain the Islamic identity, and to reinforce this awareness through various activities and educational programmes.

Thus, though most Muslim states may not be following Sharī'ah completely, a love for the Qur'ān and a love for the Prophet are still deeply entrenched in the hearts of Muslims everywhere.

?

1   What are the arguments that might be put forward in favour of and against Muslim schools?

2   What anxieties might Muslims have as they look at the contemporary world from their point of view?

3   How are Muslims attempting to deal with what they regard as western influences?

4   Why do some British Muslims want to set up their own political party? Why do other Muslims think that this is not a good idea?

5   If you were a Muslim, which of the following would you choose to do?
- join an existing political party
- join an Islamic party
- join no party.

Discuss your decision with someone who holds a different view, and listen to their arguments.

Further Reading

TEACHER'S BOOKS

Ali, Abdullah Yusuf, *The Holy Qur'ān, Translation and Commentary* (Ashraf, and other publishers, 1934)

Arberry, A.J., *The Koran Interpreted* (two vols, Allen & Unwin, 1955; or World Classics, OUP, 1964)

Asad, M., *Islam at the Crossroads* (Ashraf, 1947)

Ashraf, S.A., *Islam, Teacher's Manual*, The Westhill Project (MGP, 1988)

Al-Attas, S.M.N., *Islam and Secularism* (Kuala Lumpur, 1978)

Behishti, M.H. and J. Bahonar, *Philosophy of Islam* (Islamic Publication, USA)

Burckhardt, T., *An Introduction to Sufi Doctrine* (Ashraf, 1959)

Cragg, K., *Call of the Minaret* (OUP, 1956)

  The Event of the Qur'ān (Allen & Unwin, 1971)

Eaton, G., *Islam and the Destiny of Man* (Allen & Unwin, 1971)

Gibb, H.A.R., *Islam* (OUP, 1968)

Hamidullah, M., *The Muslim Conduct of State* (Ashraf, 1964)

Lings, M., *Muhammad* (Allen & Unwin, 1983)

Mawdudi, Abul Ala, *Towards Understanding Islam* (Islamic Foundation, 1973)

Nadwi, A.H., *A Guidebook for Muslims* (Islamic Research, Lucknow, 1985)

Nasr, Seyyed Hossein, *Ideals and Realities of Islam* (Allen & Unwin, 1975)

  Traditional Islam in the Modern World (KPI, 1987)

  Science and Civilisation in Islam (Islamic Text Society, 1987)

  Sufi Essays (Allen & Unwin, 1972)

Rahman, A., *Encyclopaedia of Seerah* (Muslim Schools Trust, 1981)

Schuon, F., *Understanding Islam* (Allen & Unwin, 1963)

Suhrawardy, A., *The Sayings of Muhammad* (J. Murray, 1941)

Taylor, M.J. and S. Hegarty, *The Best of Both Worlds* (NFER-Nelson, 1985)

Valiuddin, M., *The Qur'ānic Sufism* (Delhi, 1959)

Watson, J.L. (ed), *Between Two Cultures* (Basil Blackwell, 1978)

PUPILS' BOOKS

Hamidullah, M., *An Introduction to Islam* (IFSO, 1970)

Jameelah, M., *Islam in Theory and Practice* (Lahore, 1967)

Jeffrey, A. (ed), *A Reader on Islam* (Moulton & Co., 1962)

Nadwi, A.H. (tr. M.A. Kidwai), *The Four Pillars of Islam* (Academy of Research & Publications, Lucknow, 1972)

Tames, R., *Approaches to Islam* (J. Murray, 1982)

Students are also advised to get the following book, which gives in brief a good number of relevant quotations from the Qur'ān and Hadīth regarding all aspects of Islam:

The Seventy-seven branches of Faith by Imam al-Baihaqī, translated by Abdal-Hakim Murad, The Quilliam Press, 1990.

Glossary

Adhā, 'Id al- festival of sacrifice
adhān call to prayer
alhamdulillāh all praise be to Allah
'ālim, pl. *'ulamā'* learned person
Allāhu, or Allāh proper name for God
'amal action
'amalan sālihan good deeds
amānah the trust
al-Amīn the trustworthy
ansār 'helpers'. The title given to Medinite Muslims
   who helped the Makkan emigrants
'aqīqah naming ceremony for a child
'aql intellect
'Ashūrā' tenth day of *Muharram*
'asr, salāh al- late afternoon prayer
assalāmu 'alaikum Muslim greeting meaning
   peace be with you
āyatullāh, pl. *āyātullāh* a sign of Allah

barakah grace
Bismillāh in the name of Allah

dhikr constant remembrance
dīn obedience; submission; religion. Islam
   (submission to God) is regarded in the Qur'ān as
   al-dīn – the religion
dīn al-haqq religion of truth
du'ā' varying forms of personal prayer

fajr, salāh al- early morning prayer
fanā' annihilation or loss of self in Islamic mysticism
fard obligatory
Fātihah, Sūrah al- opening *sūrah* of the Qur'ān
fatwā legal opinion
fiqh jurisprudence; Islamic law
Fitr, 'Id al- festival to mark the end of *Ramadān*
fitrah primordial nature
fuqahā', sing. *faqīh* jurists

ghusl washing of the whole body

Hadīth a tradition or narration relating or describing
   a saying or an action of the Prophet
Hadīth Qudsī a holy tradition. The words are the
   Prophet's, but the meaning is from God by inspiration
hāfiz, pl. *huffāz* one who memorises the Qur'ān
al-hajar al-aswad the Black Stone at the Ka'ba in
   Makkah
hajj the annual Muslim pilgrimage to Makkah;
   Muslims are required to go once in their lifetime

hājjah a woman who has performed *hajj*
hājjī, pl. *hujjāz* a man who has made the pilgrimage
halāl permitted, lawful
haqīqah truth or essence
harām forbidden
Hijrah migration of Prophet Muhammad (pbuh)
   from Makkah to Medina in 622 CE
Hijrī system of dating based on the *Hijrah*
huqūq al-'ibād rights of humanity

'Id (for *'Id al-Fitr* see *Fitr*, etc.) feast, festival
'Idgāh a place for *'Id* prayer
iftār breakfast at the end of ritual fast
ihrām plain white garments worn by pilgrims to
   Makkah; the state of ritual purity
ihsān virtue, kindness, worship
ijmā' consensus of the learned among Muslims
   ('*ulamā*') on law and practice
ijtihād interpretation of Sharī'ah to solve new
   problems in conformity with divine law
'ilm knowledge
imām leader of congregational prayers
īmān faith
Injīl the Gospel revealed to the Prophet 'Īsā (Jesus)
inshā' Allāh 'if Allah wills'
iqāmah call to begin prayer
iqra' 'Read!' – a command
'ishā', salāh al- later evening prayer
ittibā' to follow

Jamā'ah, salāh bi al- congregational prayer
jihād struggle, both physical and moral
al-jihād al-akbar greatest struggle
jinn species or beings created by God from fire,
   before humans were made
Jum'ah, salāh al- Friday congregational prayer

Ka'ba 'a cube'; the sacred shrine in the Grand
   Mosque at Makkah, said to have been built by
   Adam and later rebuilt by Abraham and Isma'il
Khalīfah vice-regent of Allah; caliph; head of the
   Islamic world both spiritually and physically
khamr intoxicants, forbidden in the Qur'ān
khānqah a place of meditation for Sufis
khutbah lit. 'speech'. Usually refers to sermon given
   by the *imām* at Friday congregational prayer
kitāb book; *al-kitāb* is the Qur'ān

labbayka 'Here I am, O Lord, at your service'
lā ilāha illallāh 'There is no God but Allah'

Lailat al-Barāt   The Night of Destiny; the 15th of *Sha'bān*

Lailat al-Mi'rāj   The Night of the Ascension; the 27th of *Rajab*, when the Prophet is said to have gone to Jerusalem and visited the seven heavens, going bodily to the throne of God

Lailat al-Qadr   The Night of Power, one of the odd-numbered nights within the last ten days of *Ramadān*

madhhab   a school of jurisprudence

madrasah   college or school

maghrib, salāh al-   prayer after sunset

makrūh   'reprehensible' from the legal point of view

māshā' Allāh   what God wills

masjid   a mosque; 'the place of prostration'

mawlānā   master; member of a Sufi sect

mihrāb   niche in a mosque that marks the direction of prayer

Mīlād al-Nabī   the Prophet's birthday

minbar   pulpit in the mosque

mīqāt   place where a pilgrim to Makkah must put on *ihrām*

mi'rāj   ascension of the Prophet; see *Lailat al-Mi'rāj*

mubāh   'indifferent' from the legal point of view

muezzin, or ***muadhdhin***   one who calls to prayer

muhājirūn (pl. of ***muhājir***)   companions of the Prophet who migrated to Medina

mujāhid, pl. ***mujāhidūn***   one who fights in the path of Allah

mujtahid   one who can practise *ijtihād*, i.e. give an opinion in questions of law

mu'min, pl. ***mu'minūn***   believers in Allah; the faithful

murīd   disciple in the spiritual path

mustahab   recommended

nabī   prophet

nafs   self, soul, conscience, psyche; part of human nature

al-nafs al-ammārah   a psyche that is prone to evil

al-nafs al-lawwāmah   a soul in conflict

al-nafs al-mutma'innah   a contented psyche

niyyah   declaration of intention

qadr   belief that everything happens according to God's will

qādī   judge

qalb   heart

qiblah   direction in which Muslims must face while praying

qiyām   standing, the first posture of *salāh*

qiyās   analogy or reasoning

Qur'ān   the complete book of revelations to the Prophet

Quraysh   the dominant tribe in Makkah in the time of the Prophet

rak'ah   one unit of ritual prayers and postures

rasūl   messenger

rukū'   bowing towards the *qiblah*

sabr   patience

sadaqah   voluntary act of charity

sahābah, pl. ***ashāb***   a companion of the Prophet

sa'ī   walking between al-Safa and al-Marwah during *hajj*

salāh, pl. ***salawāt***   prescribed prayer

salām   peace – a greeting

sawm   fasting

Shahādah   the Muslim declaration of faith

Sharī'ah   law or code; Muslim Law

shaykh (or ***sheikh***)   male elder; also used as a title for Sufi leaders

Shī'a   members of a branch of Islam which separated from the orthodox *Sunnis* in 679 CE

silsilah   Sufi order

sīrah   the Prophet's life

Sūfī   Muslim mystic

Suhuf   scrolls revealed to the prophet Ibrāhīm (Abraham)

sujūd   prostration

Sunnah   practice of the Prophet

Sunnī   followers of the Sunnah of the Prophet; *Sunnīs* constitute the majority of Muslims

sūrah   chapter of the Qur'ān

tafsīr   interpretation of the Qur'ān

talbiyah   the saying of '*labbayka*' when putting on *ihrām* and entering Makkah to perform *hajj* or *'umrah*

tarāwīh, salāt al-   additional night prayers after the regular night prayers during the month of fasting

tarīqah, pl. ***turuq***   path, or the Sufi process

tasawwuf   lit. 'to put on woollen garments', i.e. to become a Sufi; the science of Sufism

tawāf al-qudūm   ritual act of walking round the Ka'ba during pilgrimage

tawhīd   unity of Allah/God

Tawrāt   the Torah, revealed to the prophet Mūsā (Moses)

'ulamā', sing. ***'ālim***   group of scholars or lawyers

ummah   community

'umrah   lesser pilgrimage to Makkah, comprising the putting on of *ihrām*, doing *tawāf* round the Ka'ba, and performing *sa'ī* between Safa and Marwah

wahy   revelation; inspiration

walī   friend of Allah

wudū'   ritual ablutions before prayer

Zabūr   the Psalms, revealed to the prophet Dāwūd (David)

zakāh   almsgiving; money due to the poor

zuhr, salāh al-   midday prayer

Index